WHAT DOESN'T KILL YOU

One Cop's Perspective on Homelessness, Mental Illness, and Addiction

Mary Beth Haile with
Eric Hofstein

ISBN-9798374259964

Library of Congress Control Number: 2018675309
Printed in the United States of America

*For my wife and children, who sacrificed
so that I could work my dream career, and
later so that I could help others.*

Thinkers think and doers do. But until the thinkers do and the doers think, progress will be just another word in the already overburdened vocabulary of the talkers who talk.

FRANÇOIS DE LA ROCHEFOUCAULD

CONTENTS

FOREWORD

At some point, Eric Hofstein decided it would be a good idea to become a police officer. He had always been drawn to law enforcement. I was not fond of the idea. I had never intended on being a "copwife". However, he clearly wanted this and if there is one thing a spouse doesn't do, it's stifle the dreams of their partner. I supported his decision.

Eric has an active mind. He is never satisfied with his current level of knowledge in a given subject. He has taken advantage of every opportunity to learn new things with the potential to make him a better cop that the departments for which he has worked could offer. It has been fulfilling for him. Eric is, perhaps above all else, a doer.

This made him proactive, and he prided himself on his aggressive police work. In those early days there was scarcely a hint of where this road would take him. There was no indication that his twenty-seven-year career would culminate in the impetus for him to write a book so that his work could continue.

When asked how he got to this point, he has no clear answer. Maybe his life was a perfect storm of early childhood influences and lifetime experiences that lead to his outreach work and the lessons he learned therewith. Maybe he is unique. I don't think so. I think his work can be replicated many times over. It is crucial that it be replicated.

Eric and I wrote this book together. I hobbled together essays from police reports, experiences he shared with me, essays he wrote and I edited, body camera footage I transcribed, and instances I witnessed firsthand. It is by necessity written in his first person narrative because this world cannot be understood any other way.

~Mary Beth Haile

BUTTERFLY EFFECT

Dispatch: "A violent woman swinging a shovel, breaking out car windows, and threatening her neighbors." Reported just days after celebrating my 46th birthday, the dispatch sounded like just another neighbor or perhaps another domestic dispute so common in that working class community that sprawled along the tributaries and inlets fed by the San Francisco Bay.

Across the street from what looked like recently strewn debris a small group of people huddled. The mix of children and adults watched intently as I approached. Their eyes flicked nervously, expectantly from the house, to me, back to the house. I walked up to the nearest neighbor, unusually calm as if she was hypnotized, staring ahead at the litter strewn house. I spoke to her, and she broke the eerie silence to confirm that the garbage was indeed the work of the woman who lived there. She had thrown oddly indiscriminate household items at people, property, and around her home before I arrived, and they had no idea why.

I crossed the street scanning the litter as I stepped

over and past it for clues as to what was taking place. Random personal items and some burnt matches failed to give me any insight as to why there was an angry female voice emanating from the rear of the house. It was the only voice, so I followed it, straining to determine whether the manic argument emitting from within was with an unseen subject, or as I ultimately determined, furiously shouted gibberish to an empty room. The former would make it a domestic disturbance, the latter an unpredictable encounter with an erratic subject with a mental health disorder.

As I approached a side gate that led to the back yard, the furious shouting was louder, and I could hear it was coming from the back of the house. Opening the gate, I cautiously walked along the side yard, minding my focus.

As the side yard emptied into the small, fenced back yard, there were more abandoned matches and several more strewn items, charred to various degrees – as if failed and discarded attempts. *Attempts at what?* Creeping up to the back door I noticed a pile of partially burned lumber and newspapers just as the overwhelming stench of gasoline assaulted me. She suddenly appeared in the doorway, each of us equally startled at the other's presence. I barked out quick orders to come outside. She answered by abruptly slamming the door shut. The smell of gasoline became overpowering as it emanated from just the few moments the door was cracked open. Backup officers began to arrive as she appeared at a window next to the door, still ranting her unintelligible tirade. It was clear she was not opening that door for anyone.

I tried the knob. Locked. I knew the gasoline fumes

would only build and become more explosive the longer that door stayed closed. There were only two possible outcomes at that point: backing away and passing on the call as a standoff situation or taking action hoping I could stop what was to come. There was no backing away to wait out a deranged and dedicated attempt to explode a house in a suburb dense with families.

I kicked in the door. Thankfully it gave in on the first attempt. Letting the momentum of my kick pull me forward, I fell into the dark curtilage of a back room, the air impossibly thick with gasoline fumes. A hint of the horror I had stepped into hit me with the sight of the floors wet with pools of gasoline, reflecting the little natural light that made it across the empty spaces form the small windows.

So startled was I by what I had stumbled into that I didn't see the more immediate danger lunging at my face. I was immediately confronted with her hands, contorted like the gnarled claws of a desperate creature. In this animalistic state, she attacked me with everything she had. I grabbed her hands to keep her from gouging at my eyes. She responded by kicking me deep in my pelvis, crushing delicate flesh against the bone. A sharp pang followed by deep, literally sickening, pain travelled upward from the testes into the gut, blinding and doubling me over. Engulfed in pain that would last for days, I struggled to maintain concentration to keep her from freeing her frenetic hands. If I allowed my focus to shift from her hands, a dam would open, letting forth the pain, rendering me unable to experience anything else. The struggle felt endless. Gasoline was slick on the floor, complicating my efforts to subdue her. I dared not use my taser for fear of ignition. All the while my heavy, deep breaths invited the noxious fumes into my lungs. I became impossibly light-headed, my breath raspy, my lungs demanding more than I could muster.

Rendered ineffective by the extremely confined space, my beat partners struggled in vain to assist, arms thrashing, until Juana and I finally lost our collective footing in the puddles of gasoline and ended up crashing onto the bed.

Finally, I could handcuff her. The door had been open long enough for the fumes to begin to dissipate, and the melee ended. My head began to clear, and I was able to take in more of my surroundings. As I led her from the house, I saw it. Is that a car battery? What are those two prongs? It dawned on me. It was an arc welder. She had been trying to ignite an arc welder, failing only because there was no power to the house. I thought again of all the burnt matches and charred debris. I wondered how long it would have taken to ignite the gas fumes, and how many times she was willing to try. She intended to burn herself to death in that house. I had just escaped the headline "HOUSE IN BAY POINT EXPLODES DUE TO APPARENT SUICIDE." The reality of my close call was washing over me as I saw the perfect Molotov cocktail placed under the gas line that went to the house near the matches. *Exactly how many people had she intended to kill today?*

I walked her to the patrol car as the crowd gawked. Families. Children. I still could not breathe freely for the fumes. I had come close to paying the ultimate sacrifice. A resentment grew. The memory of this person who almost killed me would live within me. There was a numbness to my emotional spectrum that grew in the days and weeks after the event.

That night I came home late, as I often did after a particularly eventful shift. There was much work beyond wrestling with suspects. I had to secure the scene, collect and log evidence, and interview witnesses. Determine if and what crimes were articulatable, assuring the safety of suspects, victims, fellow officers, and myself. Each responding officer had to write a clear and concise, detailed report of events, making sure that all other officers who reported on the same incident wrote factual and thorough legal documents. Edits and rewrites could take hours.

I routinely carried within me the burden of murders, suicides, child abuse, sex abuse cases, even occasional attempts on my own life. This was a seemingly simple failed suicide attempt. Though the suspect tried to light the blaze with me in harm's way, this was not the type of encounter that shook me. Yet there I was, shaken.

People in law enforcement are more intimately acquainted with suicide than one might think. There are tragic deaths, inevitable deaths, deaths like the couple who sought to add levity by drawing happy faces on the plastic bags they'd secured over their heads after connecting them to the helium tanks that had previously been used for a celebration before holding hands and taking their last deep breaths. I knew some things about people who choose this escape from life. One of those things is that women don't typically choose violent means.

Statistically men choose methods like firearms,

hanging, asphyxiation or suffocation, jumping off a bridge or cliff or out of a moving object, or using sharp objects, or vehicle exhaust gas. Women on the other hand tend to choose self-poisoning, exsanguination (such as with cutting the wrists,) drowning, hanging, and firearms, in that order[i]. Exploding one's home and potentially setting the entire neighborhood ablaze is not included in either list.

Her method was an extreme unaccounted for. She wasn't just trying to end her life. As I wrote my report of the events, a picture came into focus: it seemed she had tried to ignite increasingly incendiary items, frustration building with each failed attempt. With this she decompensated, making it that much harder for her to accomplish the goal of setting her house on fire. Her efforts escalated from random bits of flammable junk to scraps of lumber, to the arc welder and gasoline in her home and the Molotov cocktail placed under the gas line, presumably so that it would light as a result of the explosion of the gas line once she had managed to set off the explosion inside. Ironically, a lit match is often extinguished by wet gasoline before it can ignite the fumes. As her frustration grew, so did her determination to destroy her home along with her life. Everything that was her and hers was in that home. I had seen photos of family and of children I'd assumed to be hers. She was attempting to erase her entire existence.

At the time I wasn't aware of facts and statistics, but professionally I knew this was extreme. She had reached a level of pain beyond that I'd seen in the most desperate suicides. Her sheer commitment to death spurred us both into a life and death battle. I was fighting for both our lives and she, our deaths. Her attempt lit a beacon so bright as to penetrate the psychic shield I'd built; the shield that even then a part of me wanted to break down. She was attempting to annihilate herself, all her belongings, every mark she had ever made on the world. She intended to leave no trace. She mortally endangered innocents, succumbed to a pain so intense it turned her focus inward, blinding her to consequences. The neighboring families, the children, and I were just collateral damage, so desperate was she to never have been. Somewhere deep, where I couldn't yet recognize I saw her not as a suspect attacking me, but a mother with a home and a family suffering, screaming in rage against me for hindering her escape, sentencing her to continue an existence of intolerable pain, trapped in perpetual purgatory.

ERIC HOFSTEIN

11-99

Be polite, be professional, but have a plan to kill everybody you meet.

There is no such thing as routine.

The worst-case scenario is the simple code many officers will go through their entire career never hearing. It is the big red button of radio transmissions, causing everyone with a gun and badge to drop what they're doing and run lights and sirens to whomever put out the call.

I heard it that beautiful fall morning: "11-99. CHP officer down."

No matter how many times I saw CPR, it struck me as violence.

The uniform pants of the downed officer were the exact shade I wore. Neatly creased and tailored, as were mine, and nearly new in appearance, except for the road grease and detritus being mashed into it from the attempts at resuscitation. Somewhere to my side two paramedics reached into a Jeep on the shoulder and pulled a body out. It felt as if I was invisible to them. I was taken aback at the suspect's clean-cut appearance. Was I expecting something more sinister? Less than an hour before I was going about my normal routine. Now the two men barely clung to life within arm's reach of each other. If they were conscious, they could have shaken hands. It felt wrong.

I couldn't afford any emotion in this moment. I secured and preserved the crime scene, collected and logged evidence, assigned routine duties like keeping the log of all persons and things entering and leaving the scene thereby creating a time capsule for the detectives so that they have an accurate picture of what happened. Proud of my ability to step up to the plate and take responsibility in one of the worst things an officer can experience, I knew deep down it was also a way to bury emotions beneath the work.

My day was not done. 911 was pending a suspicious woman reported in the bushes in the neighborhood adjacent to the freeway I was on. It was a woman who was forced to pee in the bushes because I had blocked the freeway and other random calls for service, business as usual. Back to routine.

In the aftermath, the department sent a volunteer chaplain to sit with us in line up. He was a phone salesman who made sure to leave his business card with us before departing. Other districts had mental health days and group barbeques. The three of us in our district didn't receive so much as a check-in from the brass. We weren't even afforded the casual "how are you," that's standard procedure in work where trauma is status quo. For us it was just another day at the department.

WALK THROUGH
THE DOOR

Police officers experience an average of three traumatic experiences for every six months of service. Three traumatic encounters every six months. Year after year of service. That reality weighed on me every time I put on my uniform and walked out the door from our home to that other world.

It was a year later when I realized that I'd ceased conducting proactive traffic stops. Something was unravelling. Patrol had lost its glamor for me, and I found myself analyzing shifts in my feelings for what had been my dream career.

Two years after the murder, I received an email from an associate at the Custody Alternatives Facility.

The email described at some length the facts of the case, that she had been attempting suicide by setting herself aflame. It went on to describe her incarceration and subsequent efforts to improve her lot. She had become clean and sober and completed a behavioral health program in order to live a healthy, productive life. She was set to graduate from the program and had asked my associate to track down the officer who saved her life because she wanted to thank me. And to invite me to her graduation.

The officer who helped her. The officer who saved her. Who risked his life to protect her neighbors from the inferno with which she threatened them.

I waited two days to respond. In masculine bravado I sarcastically confirmed the subject at hand, "The chick who fought me while trying to blow up her house and gas lines at the neighbor's house. Kicked me in the gonads and then tried to claw my face while we fought in a pool of gasoline." Clearly, the anger lingered. I refused to commit an answer to the invitation, qualifying instead with an *"I'll try,"* giving myself an out in the event I could not get myself to go. I reiterated how aggrieved I was.

Ruminating, it occurred to me that perhaps I proscribed too much intent to her actions. Maybe I felt I was the only victim and did not allow enough credit to how much mental illness was to blame, making her a victim as well. Perhaps I was taking the coward's way out. It takes more effort to feel empathy than to hate. Going meant exposing myself to emotional growth. That was difficult. Avoidance was easy. Somewhere inside that ate at me, the lying to myself. Nothing invokes the conscience more than truth.

I regarded my associate's empathy. A weakness? Years later, I would feel the same abiding empathy dozens of times over. This was the beginning. She'd tossed the stone into the waters that started me on a path I could not yet see. Of the dozens of similar cases each week, why did this case move me so? The subtle ripples started silent but deep, the Butterfly Effect.

I received more emails, pleas wherein she appealed to my better nature, entreating me to take her hand and walk with her in her journey--all forwarded to me by the colleague who had advocated for her.

"... I was arrested by you. I am so grateful that you where [sic] there that day. My plans were to set myself on fire because I could not stop the voices in my head. I take full responsibility for my actions, and I want to apologize for hurting you and for my awful behavior I also apologize for not being respectful. I agree that I was out of control and did not for one moment stop to think to control myself. I was full of hate and anger I did not care about anyone at the time I had been through so much and I realize that I was taking it out on people including yourself. ... I understand that your time is very valuable and that you might be very busy and if you cannot attend I at least want you to know how I have changed my ways.

"...I want you to know my life has changed, the meaning in life changed for me, you were at the right place at the right time things had to happen the way they did so that I can be here today alive telling you my story and what I have gained in life and for you to know that I will help others recover.

"Thank you and God bless"

Maybe she was lying, conning as only a manipulative convict can do, trying to convince me to come so that the judge would see a cop advocating for her, increasing the likelihood of a favorable outcome. I could simply choose to forget the date and time and curse the name of the fellow cop who refused to let me off the hook, doggedly calling for empathy toward the person who had almost taken my life.

All this I considered.

I wore my suit. I didn't want my uniform to influence the judge at her adjudication before the graduation, and I didn't want to stand out as the cop in the room full of addicts in various stages of recovery at the following ceremony. I sat awkwardly, not knowing the etiquette of such an event. As they rose in turn to speak at the podium, I sat stoic, mindful of my expression and posture. Not wanting to display inappropriate body language, I chose to show none at all. Part of me must have known that in doing so, I sent a message about my feelings regardless.

I surveyed the room. I knew the look of addicts. The skin, the teeth, the eyes, the hair of an abused body were so familiar to me that when my eyes fell to her, I was taken aback. She looked healthy, well, clear-headed. She looked good. She *was* good.

The ceremony ended and the formality melted away as refreshments were served. I maintained my stiff posture, and she and her therapist sat with me. She had a question about the incident. Her therapist indicated it would be healing for her to hear some of the details. I obliged. At one statement, her eyes grew wide, and she was visibly shaken. She had been unaware that at one point she'd been ranting entirely in Spanish. She broke her gaze, shaken. Clearly a fight or flight trauma response had been triggered, and her therapist quickly closed in to ground her, speaking to her and gently taking her hand. I recognized something in her. Something I couldn't quantify but that I recognized. In myself? Perhaps, but that required an inappropriate amount of self-reflection for the moment. I felt my heart open. The feeling confused me. She recovered and addressed me again.

"I'll fix you a plate." An unexpected kindness, a surprising air of familiarity, an instinctive sign of caring.

She returned with two plates, setting one on the table in front of me, and the other in front of herself as she sat next to me. The only other time I was this close to her she was fighting me, a cornered wild animal raging against me, trying to kill us both. In this new moment we were connected. I found this interchange soothing, intimate. The cognitive dissonance was disorienting and disconcerting. As we broke bread, I was awash with unfamiliar emotion. We ate lunch together with an ease I didn't know how to digest. The ripples in the pond were about to carry me away into a chapter in my life that earlier I would never imagine for myself.

In retrospect, I am unsure who saved whom that day.

WHAT DOESN'T KILL YOU

19

BART

My experience at the graduation didn't negate the trauma I'd experienced months before. The officer's death weighed on me. It changed me. My once proactive policework became reactive as I initiated increasingly fewer contacts. I had seen officers like this all my career. Grizzled veteran officers reached their limit of adrenaline chasing and became completely inactive on shift until dispatched to a call. They were dubbed RODs: Retired On Duty. This was someone I swore I wouldn't become, but I was on my way. It was time to concede that my law enforcement career was ending.

Colleagues were leaving the Sheriff's Department to work for the Bay Area Rapid Transit District Police Department. A respected sergeant left. A close friend was in an officer involved shooting, and for him that trauma was impetus to leave for quieter pastures. This friend encouraged me to do the same. BART paid very well and had excellent fringe benefits. There would be no more calls to domestic violence scenes at a home where anything could be going on behind closed doors. Never again would I conduct a welfare check to find the person had been dead for days. No more calls to gang besieged neighborhoods. This would be easy money. Walk through clean stations, watch for fare evaders, ride the trains a few times a shift for high visibility.

The BART website read like a vacation brochure. A vast heavy-rail public transit system connecting five of the nine counties making up the San Francisco Bay Area, fifty stations connecting malls, tourist attractions and universities. BART patrons commute not only to San Francisco, but to outlying cities that house tech industry giants.

I sighed and turned to my wife, "So that's it. Nineteen years as a cop," I drew a deep breath, "this isn't 836 PC. 836 PC is the statute that authorizes police officer powers per state law. It's what makes a cop a cop. I'm no longer the cop I used to be. This makes it official. This is transit police. Do you know the difference?"

She did not.

"BART is a transit authority. Transit police duties are very specific. BART is 830.33."

This is what freed me from going into homes, patrolling the streets at large, and responding to any and every transgression of the law. A transit officer's purview began and ended in the transit system. This is what I wanted. This is what we wanted. But it was bittersweet. For the better part of two decades, I had adopted, for better or for worse, a specific identity. I wore it with pride, and as hokey as it sounds, had worked hard to contribute to the honor of the profession. That was done now. It was time to reinvent myself.

During my probation, I could only bid for specific

stations. Once this period passed, I would be able to bid for the station and shift of my choice. There were dozens of stations to choose from in quiet areas with varying levels of traffic. Some would allow me to spend much of my shift in a quiet office. One offered a shopping mall. I could work the rest of my days until retirement in relative peace.

My training period required me to work several different stations to familiarize myself with the system. After that, the stations for new hires were the most difficult to staff due to their low desirability. These less desirable assignments were at the Oakland and San Francisco stations where the mentally ill, the homeless, and those afflicted with addiction roamed the underground stations in search of an out of the way place to eke out a square of pavement out of the elements. Unsurprisingly, crime was high, as were commuter complaints. Just a few years earlier the opposite had been true. The San Francisco stations were coveted: clean, with access to some of the most popular areas in the city. Only the most senior officers could hope to be assigned there. As a result, the R.O.D.s took the opportunity to use them to hide until they could shuffle off to retirement. Then the opioid epidemic washed over one of the most beautiful cities in the world.

A tragedy was still unfolding as addiction gripped the most vulnerable inhabitants: those already suffering from substance use disorder or trauma that made them particularly susceptible to addiction. I had a front row seat. I also had a choice: to remain an observer, or to participate in the narrative, doing what I could to mitigate the devastation. I deliberately positioned myself to change its course.

BART in San Francisco was all foot patrol, reminding me of my childhood images of early twentieth century New York City cops walking their beats on the streets where I grew up. Unlike the original flatfoots, however, I spent twelve and a half hour shifts with twenty-five pounds of gear strapped to me as I navigated corridors peppered with blind spots and long stairwells that led to the platforms below and the streets above, a purgatory for commuters. In contrast to traditional policing, transit system work was more focused yet exposed me to a vast spectrum of cultures and lifestyles both local and global. These merged making the BART stations a melting pot through which I waded, assisting people of disparate backgrounds navigating their way through San Francisco.

In these stations, shattered lives were on display like the dioramas I once loved in New York's Museum of Natural History. Transit hallways were the anthropology section, displaying the different states of homeless people in the 21st century frozen in time. An image of any hallway or stair was an anachronism on display, revealing the condition of the society where they spent their transient existence. When the streets above became overwhelming to their deceptively delicate psyches, or they needed shelter from inclement weather to hit their dose - often a potential hot-shot - (lethal-level dose) - they trickled into the vast BART system.

Dozens of bodies in all shapes, sizes, and conditions were strewn about the marble floors. The stench of sweat and detritus was heavy. It was an underground wasteland of the human condition populated by characters from many walks of life.

The scene clashed with the uniquely American Protestant work ethic that was hardwired into me. I was shocked by this gritty world in which I found myself suddenly immersed. I had spent time in New York City and its famous subway system in my youth, but never been exposed to this level of despair. That it was an accepted part of the ecosystem of the city distressed me. There was trash on the floors and bodies everywhere. Some were clear-headed recuperating, some lounging, stoned, dying, maybe I'd come across one who had already died, discovered only because of a hallway sweep. I had seen the same theme in the inner-city gang neighborhoods as well as in the jails, but there it was sporadic. Now I saw it in the halls of a major metropolis, and it was inescapable.

I walked the hallways curious. What could have been so bad that a grimy train station floor was an acceptable alternative to whatever they left behind? Were there common themes to their stories? I knew there must have been significant crisis for them to willingly choose this lifestyle. Perhaps they weren't willing. The human mind can become accustomed to horrific environments.

I was walking law and order with no idea where to begin. I quickly realized that getting started was the most confusing part of the work. Like Groundhog Day, I walked the same corridors, day in and day out, twelve and a half hours at a time. My proscribed duties were confounded by the tumultuous world in which I found myself. There were perfunctory duties to perform but I had to navigate my way through throngs of commuters, while my previous nineteen years of training compelled me to keep my head on a swivel, monitoring the crowd for the safety of the riders and myself. Staying alert while surrounded by a constantly moving mass of people took a lot of mental and physical energy.

ERIC HOFSTEIN

BART RESIDENTS
AND REAL ESTATE

I met the schizophrenic nuclear engineer eating out of trash cans, clipping the fuzz off the edges of dollar bills, sewing the same piece of clothing over and over. Wearing a fedora and blazer, this man resembled a tenured professor who had wandered far from his university office. His obsessive-compulsive behaviors were a film loop. Occasional mutterings, venting about some scientific or philosophical principle in an argument with an unseen opponent were the only variants.

The Ethiopian orphan who lost his parents to the A.I.D.S. epidemic in Africa lived in the station and called the officers his friend. His mind was failing in some subtle, sophisticated way that enabled him to present appropriately in casual contacts, but once I spent any amount of time with him, it was clear that something was off. Over time, I learned he had come from a beautiful home and adopted family who loved him. He was a gifted soccer player and a good student. One day, unexpectedly, he walked out the door away from stability into chaos, homelessness, and addiction. He would ingest whatever he could, self-medicating for some undiagnosed ailment. One epidemic had fed into another, but the latter had no slogans or celebrity charities. "Silence = Death" was created to bring a voice to the A.I.D.S. crisis. But what is the opioid victim's slogan, the phrase that brings us together to fight for those afflicted with Substance Use Disorder? Where is their bumper sticker? The orphan needed to hear it.

The haunting baritone, classically trained to project across vast auditorium spaces, reverberated with a rare quality, filling the tiny corridors. A siren of the land, he called to travelers imploring "feel my sadness, my loss, come to me." So stunned by his voice were some that they would momentarily freeze to determine if that beauty was coming from some unseen radio - or rather the hunched figure crammed into a walker with a microphone, the wire an umbilical cord feeding nutrients from his past to the small speaker. Occasionally the quiet applause of a single listener, followed by the clink of coins landing in the tip cup. Other times a person would break their gaze hypnotized by the loveliness and temporarily distracted from their original pressing business. The performer's body broken from a harsh life of homelessness; he traded the top shelf whiskey of affluence for the easily accessed opiates of the street. This singer had once fetched top dollar for his operatic concerts, now performing for free in the obscure underground of a San Francisco BART station.

I learned the nuances of station real estate over time the same way one might gaze at a complicated painting full of detailed images and suddenly see something never previously noticed: a line, a color, a small image.

I conducted sweeps in the train stations the way I had done cell checks in the jail modules. I made routine rounds to check on the welfare of the people inhabiting the system, and the facility itself for signs of damage or danger. In this way, performing my duties had the added benefit of avoiding unwanted administration scrutiny or supervisor attention. A built-in alarm clock developed quickly, "Crap, we better go do a sweep before Sarge gets cranky. I'll finish this report later."

Eventually my sweeps made me experienced with the finer details of nooks and crannies throughout my station. This was essential because of the mentally ill people who wandered into the system, sometimes looking for temporary reprieve, sometimes permanent refuge from the outside world, sometimes for a secluded place to die. They crawled into walled ducts, burrowed into paneled ceilings, broke into secured hidden rooms that only those with detailed knowledge of the sprawling underground areas housing conduits and emergency escape sections knew about. A call from a group of engineers who had accessed a rarely used closed section to find a transient person was not uncommon. Many, even seasoned, officers did not know about these areas. There were small, secured corridors bisecting the two opposing train tunnels, power control rooms, and rooms whose purpose I couldn't fathom, much less know why they were placed deep in the bowels of system. "Anybody know where control room A-26 is at?" The officers didn't have maps. They didn't even know if there were current maps. Verbal directions from dispatch were often the only option to find hidden areas. Like post-apocalyptic depictions of forgotten tunnels in the New York subway system, BART had its share of corridors into which the city's invisible citizens could chose to disappear.

As I walked the stations conducting a sweep, I was in a three-dimensional maze searching for the smallest asymmetrical lump. It could be a person, random items, or both. The arbitrary nature of these easter egg hunts was so bizarre I began collecting images of odd finds: a paper bag with mannequin heads, a suitcase full of spilled gels and liquids, an electronic device with strings and wires sticking out and tied together like a small child's art project.

When I discovered a person, it always amazed me how small they could make themselves appear, how contorted they could get when burrowed into spaces not designed to contain a living body. It was an ability enhanced by narcotics that can make the muscles and tendons incredibly flaccid and flexible. They were immune to any signals from the body indicating pain or damage. Another byproduct of the dissociated mind.

I used contextual signs to recognize the benign from objects that could injure or kill. For this reason, everything was examined. Sometimes I'd find something that resembled an Improvised Explosive Device. A night of busy hands during a methamphetamine high routinely created something that in sobriety even the architect couldn't explain. All memory of their effort was lost as their mind rambled on with discombobulated thoughts. In their wake they left meth induced detritus for the BART employees to find.

MISKA

Reminiscent of a professor lounging between classes, Miska fed her voracious appetite for intellectual novelty. She read the newspaper every day. It was a routine that gave her respite from the stress of the world at large. The day I met her, there was a particularly fascinating article highlighting the newest neurological research. She sat in the BART station amid the bustle of people going to and fro, seeing only her paper neatly quartered and tented displaying the article in question.

Truth be told, she craved the intellectual stimulation from these articles. Highly intelligent, she followed her high school graduation role as valedictorian with earning four letters at an Ivy League university. She found a way to explore her many and varied interests from science to the arts, via jobs involving the type of hard labor usually reserved for men much larger than her petite frame might conjure. The embodiment of the women's movement, she proved that a woman certainly could do anything a man could do.

She sat so that her paper rested at perfect reading

height, her stylish glasses perched just far down enough on her nose to read comfortably without tilting her head. It was in this manner that I saw her. Intrigued at her striking appearance, I approached her, introduced myself, and asked what reading had her so captivated. She shared with me the subject matter, and we struck up a conversation. Soon enough we were having a detailed conversation about neurology, specifically prions. It was emerging science, and we shared a fascination with it. The whole conversation would have been unremarkable in a university faculty office or student union. This woman did not belong here, in this situation.

I gently tried to steer the conversation to learn more about her, but the moment she got the inkling it was becoming personal, she became guarded. As the conversation moved further from prions to the personal realm, her responses became canned, as if ruminated on continuously for some time. I tried to elicit information without spooking her, emotionally dialing in, reading her as much as she was reading me. I had to keep her engaged and talking. I was as intrigued as I was concerned and wanted to know more about what brought her here. There is training on how to speak with people, give information, but there is no training on how to go out into the world and empathically connect with people. I was learning now. Eventually I learned that her family had ostensibly barred her from access to her money. She was resistant, still I pushed. I had to know. Who was she? Where had she come from, and why? More and more Miska spoke non sequiturs. I patiently and earnestly listened, waiting for the hint that would betray her true story. Surely that family was somewhere suffering from her absence.

It was obvious to me that Miska just wanted to read her paper in peace. This was her safe place, with her newspaper, deep in her mind, ruminating on scientific discoveries, distracted from her past misadventures. Still, I persisted. As much as I tried to coax actionable personal information from her, she outwitted my attempts. She was clearly brilliant, clearly drawing on a lifetime of rich and varied experiences. This woman was an enigma, and she fiercely guarded her secrets. These were hers alone, a world within herself, Miska the only inhabitant. She not only preferred it this way, she had painstakingly created this world to protect herself from the insults offered up by the world at large. And here I came clumsily barreling my way in, for what reason? What need had I for her or her for me? Just her paper, just her paper. That was all she needed. I could kindly see my way to someone somewhere who surely needed my services. My questions were pedestrian, and she had no reason to trust me beyond the uniform. I responded by literally stepping back to test the limits of her boundaries. Creating physical space was a way to afford her a sense of safety and autonomy. Now my investigative brain was in overdrive. I could have, should have just walked away to attend to my myriad law enforcement responsibilities. She wasn't causing trouble in the system. She was minding her own business. But I couldn't shake the fact that she was out of place here.

Here she sat, well dressed and well kempt, obviously highly intelligent, reading a newspaper on the BART hallway floor, legs out in front of her among the roaches, the rats, the urine and feces human and otherwise, eking out a world for herself among the lost as the dense commuter crowd, often peppered with the aged and infirm, struggled to navigate around her. What should I do for her? What could I do for her? She had no interest in participating in any efforts on her behalf. Professional protocol called for removal from the floor. I wondered, though, if that was a real solution. I was faced with the choice of the seemingly obvious, to perform my perfunctory law enforcement duty, and the seemingly impossible, to coax enough information from her to get her help to leave the filthy station floor among the growing homeless population in varying states of decompensation. I could see that something was off. She was psychiatrically decompensated, but not on the level of Juana. Not on the level of the man who shot the CHP officer. I could not hold her based on what I was witnessing.

In California, the colloquial term for the statute is 5150. It affects a law that allows the author; a police officer, emergency room physician or psychiatrist; to hold the subject against their will in the event they are a danger to themselves, others, or gravely disabled. In effect, it revokes some of their constitutional rights, and cannot be taken lightly. I was not one to write a 5150 on a person unless I was sure that was the only way I could help them. Being sheltered was not legally considered a basic need, even for children, and she was clearly well fed, well dressed, and looked healthy. Neither could I leave her in her current state. Conventional wisdom had no resolution for Miska's problem. She was not in danger, nor did she have any desire to change her circumstance. To ignore her wishes was to betray her agency. To ignore her diminished quality of life was to concede that she needn't enjoy the fullness of her previous life. Here I stood with a decision to make.

I would not walk away. When I asked in my naivete about the possibility of a homeless shelter, she scoffed. She had been to a shelter. There, as she attempted a shower, a simple act to return some humanity after being on the streets, a man had stripped naked and entered the shower with her. Shelters were not only unsafe, but filthy, full of all manner of parasite including bedbugs, which were possibly the most difficult to rid oneself of. If I tried to connect her with any of the social service programs available, they would assuredly try and fail to get her into a shelter, try and fail to get her to psychiatric services, which require the client to make and manage a schedule based on the nine-to-five world of office hours that did not apply to those living on the floors of transit stations in a safety of their own making. She was not motivated to be anywhere else. She would sit here and read her paper. Thanks, but no thanks, she had built her world.

As I carefully prodded, I provoked short rants where shining nuggets from which I could glean the faintest of clues were revealed. I spoke, listened, and waited. There! She mentioned the name of her hometown. There! The name of a lawyer. In her ramblings, I could discern nuggets of reality. I clung to them. I would apply the investigative skills of a career in law enforcement to Miska's case in a way that I had never encountered.

In this moment I would resolve to reimagine my role. I would reinvent what it meant to be a law enforcement officer who waded into the muck with the desperate and alone, pulling them with me as I trudged out onto solid ground. I must decide if I was up to the task that so many – so many people, organizations, cities, state governments and entire countries—had failed: how to help the most vulnerable, third world to first world, suffering from a social crisis that struck without prejudice.

Once she had had enough of me, she left on her own, giving me an out. I returned to the office to quickly note the few details I was able to glean. It was like looking at a jigsaw puzzle with missing pieces. Her name, her hometown, and her father's attorney. In front of me I had a mystery. Without a crime, standard police operations were off the table. I had to reimagine my role. Using the tools available to any private citizen, I performed an exhaustive internet search and found a law firm in that town associated with a lawyer with that surname. Without much hope, I left a message. To my surprise, the attorney returned my call. He had retired years prior, but the message had somehow reached him and upon hearing Miska's name, he was compelled to reach out. He had been the family attorney for decades and knew them quite well. They had been looking for her. He promised to forward my information, and here began the resolution of my first case.

ERIC HOFSTEIN

SAN FRANCISCO

San Francisco sits on a peninsula that juts out into the deep waters at the eastern edge of the Pacific Ocean. Walking about the city, a deep chill transcends the physical. It embeds itself in the psyche with the familiarity that increases as one navigates the city. Damp cold from deep trenches of the frigid waters of the surrounding bay marry with the warmer dry land to produce a blanket of fog sometimes so thick that driving becomes dangerous. From across the bay, it looks as if clouds have been rendered immune to gravity. It is an emotionally triggering cold, unaffected by warm clothing and the distracting elation that comes from experiencing an iconic city. It sprawls, settling on the unprepared visitor with a crypt-like chill.

For many, this is an acceptable price to pay for the uniquely San Franciscan lifestyle. It offers post card worthy landscapes, rolling hills and sidewalks so steep, they have built-in stairs and architecture whose preservation is embedded in the city's culture. The roads of the Sunset District are bisected by street cars and lined with hilly waves of neatly kept Victorian homes that sacrifice yard space for housing footage. Squeezed

ERIC HOFSTEIN

together into tight knit old-world landscapes, it is common to stare with squinted eyes, imagining the same view through the eyes of San Franciscans 100 years earlier. Historic exteriors with restored sconces, molding, and lattices finessed with an artist's detailing emerge from tree lined scenes that seem to rise up from the surrounding bay. A vintage backdrop stretches out from redwood trees to the beach creating an eclectic mix of style and geography.

The culture reflects the enigma that is the Golden City. In a single day, a resident can attend a drum circle, high mass at Grace Cathedral, and Shabbat at one of the many beautiful Synagogues. In the evening, perhaps take in the opera, a nightclub featuring jazz greats at Bix, a rave at a location disclosed only to the invited or try their hand at a not-so-underground sex club featuring the kink of their choice. Wrap it up with three a.m. pancakes at Little Orphan Andie's. Everyone loves Little Orphan Andie's. They might return to the Castro district for some boutique shopping the next afternoon if the malls or downtown department stores aren't to their liking. Of course, there are many neighborhoods with boutique lined streets to choose from, each with their own genre.

Anti-consumerists are a large part of San Francisco, as well. They can be found hiking in the deceptively large Golden Gate Park, which stretches from the end of the Haight/Ashbury district to the Pacific Ocean. The Presidio is a decommissioned army base built in 1891, where they can still climb on and around concrete batteries added as anti-aircraft defense during WWII. Among the beautiful if invasive Eucalyptus trees, the city is forgotten as they find themselves at the base of the Golden Gate

Bridge, the deceptively gently lapping waves masking the infamously rough waters that served as the primary deterrent for escape from Alcatraz.

Homes in and around San Francisco are highly sought after. The smallest, most humble San Francisco houses easily sell for over a million dollars. It is so appealing that free spirited drifters come to San Francisco from far and away for the opportunity to live on the very streets.

More than beauty draws people to the pricey homes and beautiful bay of San Francisco. The heart of Silicon Valley, with high paying jobs, is easily commutable by BART. Tech companies tempt potential employees to the Bay Area with offers of cash towards the purchase of a house and luxury charter busses to mitigate the deterrent of commuting in the second worst traffic in the nation. This puts these mostly Midwest and Southern transfers in competition with wealthy locals in order to get their piece of the historical forty-nine square mile city. As a result, there is a relatively new phenomenon of old money clashing with new, creating a perfect storm of culture war fueled growing pains.

With more millionaires per capita than anywhere else in the world, it is a strange mix of opulent wealth styles. Sometimes called limo liberals or blue jean millionaires, they're known for their liberal politics and causal lifestyles. The city across the bay, Oakland, is the birthplace of the Black Panther Party and the careers of activists like Huey Newton and Bobby Seale. Adjacent Berkeley's People's Park has been at the epicenter of counterculture since 1967. At the same time, the Haight/Ashbury district in the city has offered refuge to people of varied and disparate cultures, self-described hippies escaping their 1950s bourgeois existence, all weaved together in a tapestry of free love. These varied archetypes come together in a Venn diagram, the center of which is drug experimentation.

While the sociopolitical climate of the San Francisco Bay Area has evolved in its attitude surrounding drug use and Substance Use Disorder, many areas around the country still hold the user accountable for circumstances wildly outside of their control. This makes San Francisco as desirable a sanctuary for those suffering the repercussions of the drug culture that the city helped create, as for those seeking that culture itself.

I had lived in San Francisco briefly in the late 1980s with my then fiancée. I was returning to an entirely different city.

DR. JECKYLL AND
MR. HYDE

I learned that addiction does not discriminate based on means, race, culture, or religion. When I started outreach work, I held sanctimonious preconceived notions and antiquated, simplistic views. Growing up in the sixties and seventies in the Northeast left me with a harsh set of opinions. There were good people, and then there were crooks, skells, and junkies. These characterizations are inaccurate and inappropriate, just like my obsolete and myopic opinions. Over time doing outreach work, after descending into the chasm with hundreds of homeless addicts, I grew into a more empathetic and balanced set of beliefs. In return for being more objective and open minded, I became better at my work enabling me to do more and to be more efficient at helping people. It was a butterfly effect. My outreach work affected the addicts as much as they affected me. My empathy grew and became easier to evoke in even the toughest cases. I would climb into that hole with them and feel their trauma and pain.

I dug into my outreach efforts to discover the

foundations of each homeless addict's condition. I found that when I understood these people better and felt the source of their addiction, I was profoundly more effective with my approaches, interactions, and resource assistance.

Empathy is more than listening. It is a shared endeavor. It is climbing down into the dark abyss with another human and taking in all the stimuli, breathing it in and *living their suffering with them.* My goal was to climb out of the abyss while pulling them out with me, at least far enough to remind them of their humanity

Addiction is a symptom of pain: physical, psychological, and/or emotional; and often rooted in trauma. It is born of these pains. It weaves itself deep into the core of our personalities until the biochemistry and hardwiring of our brains are changed. What doesn't kill you doesn't necessarily make you stronger. Often it leaves you tattered and bleeding, a fractured shard of your former self. We see it in our mental hospitals, emergency departments, rehab facilities, and on the city streets we walk to and from work, shopping, and play with blinders, moving through the discarded to navigate our best lives.

Addiction is often a form of self-medicating. The results can be starkly visible. I would fixate on the before and after pictures of many of the people with whom I worked. In addition to dramatic physical changes, the addict may start to exhibit sudden shockingly noticeable behaviors that grow with their usage and form habits: picking and digging at the skin, shuffling of weight from one foot to the other, jaw clenching and other physical ticks and sudden movements, as well as the disorganized, pressured, or slow and slurred speech, drooping eye lids, and hunched posture. Mood swings may spiral into sudden rages and spiteful language that leaves one wondering if they are dealing with a stranger possessed.

Eliciting cooperation is difficult, and the longer they are on the streets the more trauma they suffer. Many people I tried to help initially balked at my offers, choosing instead to live street medicated in a chemically induced bliss. Caseworkers begged me to reach out to a person whose family feared he could lose his life to the sepsis that infected his leg. He was offered a trust in excess of $1,000,000 to complete a thirty-day stint in rehab. He declined. Instead of giving up on them, I respected their choices while evaluating how much of that decision was made by the monster inside, and how much came from the person.

In 1886 Robert Louis Stevenson had a nightmare that made him think about the duality of man. His allegorical novella The Strange Case of Dr. Jekyll and Mr. Hyde examines the unremitting presence of a darker self carried by all people. In the novella, the protagonist ingests an unknown chemical mixture to summon his baser self, who commits heinous acts while in control of their mutual body.

As I grew into my work and developed the ability to see the complexities and nuances in people I met, Dr. Jekyll and Mr. Hyde came to mind. In my outreach, most of the time I was working with this duality: Jekyll possessed by Hyde. Hyde is every addict. He is the alcoholic, drug addict, the gambler, the hoarder, the thrill seeker, the sex addict; and he is the workaholic.

"He is not easy to describe. There is something

wrong with his appearance; something displeasing, something down-right detestable. I never saw a man I so disliked, and yet I scarce know why." –Robert Louis Stevenson.

In the world of Substance Use Disorder, the monster Hyde wants to do drugs and doesn't care if it kills them both. That is how the monster works, it is simplistic, primitive, and living in the ancient part of the brain all animals have, where base instincts lie and the need for survival stands at the ready, always on guard. Hyde grows more powerful every moment it is in control, entwined in the survival mode of the limbic system.

Hyde's survival mode is perpetually awake and in complete control. He hijacks thought and chemical responses as he shares mortality with the same corporeal shell as Jekyll. But Hyde is incredibly unstable and easily triggered into the red at the slightest provocation. To Hyde, anything that gets in the way of the next hit is a provocation. The more time between its drug hits, the closer to withdrawals it gets, the more provoked it gets, and the closer to death it feels.

As it feels death closing in, the effects of the powerful synthetic drugs explode the host into discombobulated thoughts and sometimes completely disconnected sense of reality. This can last for hours to days, or sometimes weeks to months. With methamphetamine users this is commonly referred to as meth psychosis. In a psychedelic alternate reality, the drugs push the body into an internal chaos making Hyde lose all ability to maintain mental and physical homeostasis. In this state of skewed emotions, false and dangerous priorities form, and children, parents, jobs, hobbies, sanity may be shed from Hyde's psyche. Those things are luxuries for Hyde at best, a provocative hinderance to getting more drugs at worst. Provoked enough, Hyde may even see family and friends as an antagonist hindering the endeavor to get what feels to him like the only medication for physical and psychic survival.

There is no communicating with Hyde, it is a single-minded creature obsessed with feeding its addiction. It is the monster that steals from family, abandons its children, lies, and makes false promises to change. As a teen it will sneak out a window and steal its parent's car in the middle of the night. As an adult it will ignore obligations, and as a parent it will abandon children. When confronted it will wail, pitch fits, cry, threaten, emotionally extort, and make promises as long as you give it what it wants in the moment. It has no future, so it doesn't care. Hyde can also be very disarming with charm; it knows your weak points and exploits your love for Dr. Jekyll with wanton disregard.

It's easy to hate Hyde. Hyde destroys everything it touches, the reason for all the pain and suffering of everyone involved. The family hates Hyde. The therapist, the emergency room doctor, and the cop, the neighbors, even the pastor at the soup kitchen hate Hyde. How many times are we told love the sinner, hate the sin? But you cannot hold hate for one without tainting the other.

I learned to wait for Dr. Jekyll to appear. When he did, I would coax him out. I built Jekyll up, reminding him of his place in the world and his dreams and offered my support to accomplish them again. I would not indulge Hyde, rather coax out Jekyll. Always supporting one without enabling the other, strengthening the one so that the other could no longer pull him back in. I would not hold Jekyll accountable for Hyde's actions. Hyde is the millstone wrapped around Jekyll's neck, keeping him moored to the trauma that perpetuates the cycle of his addiction. Hyde will always be there, clawing at Jekyll. The latter's confidence must be constantly strengthened, his ego nurtured, so that he can maintain control. This is the cycle of addiction, recovery, and relapse.

It was here I learned the two most important aspects to improving a homeless addict's life: motivation and timing. A key factor was developing incentive for them to want to get better. I regard a twist on an adage, a favorite of my beat partner Dave, "You can lead a horse to water, but you cannot make him drink. However, you can make him thirsty." I set out to make them thirst for life.

Without both motivation and timing, outreach work will fail.

Hyde is unpredictable, he emerges and is then energized by any variety of factors. All I could hope for was to see patterns and cycles while looking for telltale signs of familiar behaviors. Like a weather caster without radar information, there were possibilities and likelihoods of what was to come, but no knowns or absolutes. That is why it was so imperative to always be as ready as possible to meet them where they were, to help them take the next step up the harm reduction ladder. Readiness and preparation for their next step once Jekyll appears is the key to progress in homelessness and addiction. In order to accomplish this, I had to dig deep into their personal stories and determine what their primary drives behind the motivations were. It may have been pain, trauma, a mental health disorder, or a combination of any of these. Knowing the people intimately was the key to building true bonds and real engagement that would help me determine an individualized methodology.

I needed a way to influence temptations and cravings that had a domino effect on their motivations and behaviors. The goal was to make Jekyll want something more than Hyde wanted his drugs. Sometimes it was an impossible endeavor, so compromise was common. That may look like managing my own expectations and accepting grim realities. Not everyone wanted to change, and some did not want their Hyde to relinquish control. Empowering Jekyll would often lead to a mewling Hyde, clawing at flesh as he raged just below the consciousness for his next fix. There is an emotionally numbed equanimity that comes with capitulation to Hyde and his drug barraged mind.

Conceding capitulation however often meant watching a steady decline, like a slow suicide. It drained my fortitude and enthusiasm until the hopelessness defeated me. This was a blow to doing outreach work that is already so inherently emotionally draining.

As I ruminated on this, feeling the tinges of burnout growing, I once asked Will if I was actually helping. I liked Will and with his constant cycle of overdoses, recoveries, and relapses, I really felt like he was spinning his wheels. I wondered if anything I had done for Will went beyond superficial conversations and joking together. Will said that talking with me, my beat partner Dave, and his case workers was particularly important to him. Besides the motivation it gave him and the sense of self-worth that comes from social engagement and being worthy of another person's time, Will said every moment he was talking with us was a moment he wasn't going to look for his next hit. His Jekyll controlled the moment and Hyde was locked in the bell jar, still there, still pining away, destined to get out, but not in that moment.

Those afflicted with addiction crave positive attention and that, juxtaposed with the volatility of their chaotic behaviors, affects their relationships with family and friends evoking lies, false promises, and betrayal. I expected to encounter the volatile, obstinate behaviors I had seen when answering 911 calls. But when working with people who were not in the midst of crisis but instead stoned and miserable in a dark alley, I met Jekyll.

When these sons and daughters, mothers and fathers, people who were once children full of potential and awe peeked around at the world outside the abyss, I worked with them to develop their self-esteem in ways that built hope and loosened the vice grip in which their pain, shame, and guilt held them. That shame and guilt cycle knocked them into that chasm initially was a continual barrier to their recovery. Shame and guilt fed Mr. Hyde, affecting their will to climb out. Beating back that shame and guilt enabled them to see a future, gave them hope for a healthier and happier existence, and the dignity to believe they were worthy of it.

When I got on their level to meet them where they were, I would feel a powerful urge to 'fix' them. I felt a panic at the naturally plodding pace of progress, and in some moments, I felt useless to help in any meaningful way. Time can be the enemy with opiate, amphetamine, and hallucinogen dependence. A person can easily reach a point where they are one hit away from permanent damage or death. This results in many helpers and professionals becoming too pushy and losing rapport. That is not empathy. Because of this, often helpers, case workers, cops, lawyers and other professionals dive into outreach work with good intentions but failed results.

The helper becomes hyper focused on what they want to do, not what the person they are working with needs. The addict in turn may get so much attention, that the attention becomes the primary focus. Here, for the helper, disappointment becomes as familiar as it is devastating. Caught up in the dysfunctional lonely world of addiction and homelessness and disconnected from friends and family, they crave emotional connection and interaction.

They need to feel someone cares about them and form sudden, intense, and often violent relationships with other addicts, sharing in their disease with volatile passion. It is then easy, as they walk the fine line between harm reduction and enabling, for the helpers to fall into the pit with the addict, participating in their descent into death.

San Francisco is a city wrought with contradictions that marry together like the frantically changing incongruent scenes in a fever dream. Unlikely narratives pull the fitful sleeper from one story the next, at once nonsensical and deeply profound. I was pulled along into the deepest nightmares and most hopeful dreams of the people I touched for five years. I was deeply involved in their worlds, and just as those literally drowning often pull their rescuers into the water to share their fate in their efforts to climb out, so would those figuratively drowning on the asphalt of the City by the Bay threaten to drag me under.

Exposure to varied and disparate experiences, immersive learning, spurs the growth of new neuronal pathways. It requires willful effort to not change one's outlook when exposing oneself to the lives of others. I had many moments of clarity in my years with the forgotten of San Francisco. Not only those I was able to help, but every person who avoided my gaze, every person I stepped over to reach another who begged for help, every desperate parent, sibling, child who implored me had a profound affect. My work wasn't the result of a conscious decision, or a resolve to be part of what is good and right in the world. It became simply what I did. One person at a time, I was herded from the wide swath of patrol to the narrow path of search and rescue.

ERIC HOFSTEIN

SEARCHING
FOR RIVER

Early in my outreach efforts I went looking for a young girl after my shift ended. She had disappeared from her usual haunts and her mother reached out, pleaded with me in a desperation that only a parent could truly appreciate. I knew River. Meeting her mother only reinforced a connection. To walk away from such a primal appeal for help would have left me with such guilt wrenched sleeplessness, that answering her plea was the better choice, regardless of my personal needs. That began the slow erosion of personal boundaries when doing this work. Years into retirement I continued to struggle with the question: how far was too far, and what was "the right choice?"

I had mixed feelings about changing my routine commute time to search for an abused homeless young addict somewhere in the drug infested areas of the city.

I was out of my comfort zone without my visible police identity in their realm, during the work shift of the underworld. It was dark and cool in the pacific coast early fall night, as those of the daytime world from which they had been ejected were winding down with friends and family. It was the most active time of day for homeless addicts. Here, I was the outsider. Early in my career the old timers used to say that anyone wandering around in those late-night hours was reasonably suspicious and up to no good, because "normal people" were in bed sleeping.

I took the train route I had spent the previous twelve and a half hours traversing in a police uniform, now in civilian clothes and feeling vulnerable, stripped of my protective armor. I was not worried for my personal safety, rather about what I may witness and be forced to intervene in, distracting from the task at hand and necessitating an explanation about why I was there. I did advise my supervisors, but the body language and the hesitation in their initial responses betrayed what a full explanation of any incident would look and feel like. The wrong off duty situation could cause a backlash, shutting down my on-duty outreach work as well. I had experienced this before working professionally risky projects. Direct supervisors are by and large nervous creatures caught between upper-level leadership and responsibility for their subordinates. There was a level of trust between good supervisors and subordinates: they let out the proverbial leash as long as activities didn't cause administrative scrutiny of their leadership skills, especially if they had an eye on promotional opportunities. I did not want to violate that trust and the flexibility my supervisors afforded me. They were remarkably understanding and even supportive of my work, and I did not want that to change.

That night I exited the elongated escalator from

the BART station into the heart of the city's drug culture and my senses heightened, my head on a swivel as I maneuvered through the crowds avoiding eye contact, mimicking the familiar drug shuffle, rather than employing the usual command presence strides of a foot patrol cop. Surrounded by the red cement squares stretching hundreds of yards in each direction, I focused on my mission.

The United Nations Plaza is an international beacon in front of San Francisco's city hall where those who live their lives outside the boundaries of society gather as the workday of the city shuts down and the night life ramps up. Created to offer a welcoming atmosphere for visiting dignitaries, the plaza is sometimes adorned with flags from many nations, a testament to the prestige of San Francisco. At the same time, city workers clean up an estimated 3,000 dirty needles every month, despite efforts to provide safe disposal systems for users. A person who is virtually unconscious, on the nod from injecting drugs, does not seek out a $20,000.00 trash can for the sake of public safety.

A massive stone lined fountain sits off to the side, during the day filled with seagulls and bathing homeless and "tweakers" stripped down and enjoying the cold water on their skin that has been heated by the effects of the methamphetamine. Some have lost touch with reality, screaming at invisible entities and indiscriminately throwing anything not bolted to the ground.

Near the darkened corners of the fountain is a small walkway leading into the edges of the formal

Tenderloin low-income housing units. Here small packs of bay area black marketeers buy the wares addicts have shoplifted. Quickly shuffling around with their unique herky-jerky gait, losing patience as they seek buyers for items they carry and even drag along. These items are quickly evaluated based on the clientele of the buyer, each focused on specific products at specific price points, and knew they held an advantage over the desperate people who would take any amount of money to afford at the very least enough of their drug of choice to get them to the next hit. The San Francisco Black Market was underway.

The famous Billy Graham Civic Auditorium was framed by a line of young people snaking around the building. Knowing that the theatre often hosted outreach events that offered services to the homeless, it struck me that the woman I was looking for was likely to be there. As I began to scan them, it was quickly apparent that I would not find River in this crowd. These were clearly concertgoers in line to enter the theatre. I noticed figures across the street, away from the lights of the theatre, and assumed they were concertgoers, tipping one back to loosen up for the performance.

I turned away from the crowd under the lights of the theatre back toward the darkness and headed across the street. As I approached the gloom, as if crossing some threshold into the macabre, faces and figures became abruptly clear and I saw that most were in various stages of narcotics use: some were completely passed out, some looked like they were dancing on deaths doorstep, and others were actively injecting with furious focus. I saw people working their rigs; cooking, preparing, or cleaning as if they were at work and happily focused on a favorite hobby, project hands working, eyes moving furtively, lips smacking.

It looked like a centipede of humanity snaking down the sidewalk that rimmed the front portion of City Hall. The only illumination was from a few sulfur tinged streetlamps, adding to the eeriness of the horror show in which I found myself. The head of the centipede was the healthiest, and was thereby the most affected by the powerful narcotics they injected. The first in the process of hitting, his thigh was exposed as he focused on keeping the needle tip steady in the vein. The next was lying face up, his syringe dangling form the needle still inside his leg. In the direct glare of the streetlight above us, I could see the syringe plunger was not fully depressed. He was a new user. So affected by the initial hit of narcotics squirted into his bloodstream that he passed out before he could finish. His body flaccid in the folding chair commonly used at outdoor events, his arms spread wide, fingers inches form the ground, he lay locked in a pose as if patiently waiting for his heavenly embrace into eternal peace. The scene reminded me of renaissance paintings of victims in the throes of a plague, twisted in various poses of slow death.

Advancing, I stumbled upon a haunting scene: a young woman, her face still healthy looking compared to her peers, held a mirror under the dim streetlamp, consumed in concentration, her aim to inject into a vein in her neck. The image horrified me. New users don't typically shoot up into the neck. This indicated to me that her addiction hit her so hard and so fast that her peripheral veins had already shut down. Shooting into the larger veins of the neck was the last-ditch effort of a long term, hardened addict, because the drugs eventually destroy the smaller veins in the body. Her focus was so singular, there was no danger of her recognizing my presence standing within arm's reach of her.

This woman exposed to me a truth that vindicated my fears and informed my work going forward. I had the sickening realization that the crowd in the light and the crowd in the dark were the same beyond the conflicting veneers of filth and makeup. One side of the street, a chaotic mass of bodies beaten, trampled, discarded and forgotten. Across the narrow city road, a tidy, symmetrical queue of young people clean, pressed, happy and literally sparkling with glitter and jewelry, dressed for a night out at a legendary venue. The same age groups, the same focus, and the same expectation of that night's events; but one would be delivered by a syringe and a dirty, bent needle, and the other by a clean, machine processed ticket; the tools of admission both offering the same dopamine high.

Here, immersed and drowning in their collective despair, drug fumes in the air, trash and humanity indiscriminately strewn at my feet, I felt myself becoming overwhelmed. As I felt my focus being wrenched from my mission, "Hey officer." An uncharacteristically casual greeting. In the daylight, Matt was hostile with law enforcement, harassing patrons until they were forced to call for help. Matt had a mental health disorder and was a heavy drug user. He was all about "FUCK THE PO-LICE." A regular to BART PD, our encounters when I was on duty were always confrontational. Tonight, however, Matt approached me with a friendly familiarity. In Matt's element, here at night with the others of his tribe, rather than he in mine in the daytime with the city awake and buzzing around them, changed the dynamics. Perhaps he was just happy to see a familiar face. I was surprised, and a little taken aback, that I was so easily recognized in the dark, out of uniform, my hoodie obscuring most of my face.

As if Matt's greeting pinged some sort of ally GPS, Will approached from behind cradling his still smoldering crack pipe, at once overjoyed at my presence and feeling the weight of the shame and guilt cycle. In my relatively brief time working with these people, I came to see many as my kids. These kids essentially vetted me to the extremely suspicious community, and I was pegged as an advocate. Will was drawn like a moth to this beacon of hope, a tether to his former humanity. He followed me for a time, sobbing as he hit the pipe he clutched, flooded with remorse over the loss of his daughter. I knew that Will had lost his beloved daughter as a direct result of his dependence on crack. The abiding pain of losing his child, the anguish that ate at his soul like acid to flesh, could only be mitigated by that damned drug. I looked into Will's eyes as the tears poured forth. There was nothing to be said, nothing to be done. Will was trapped. He could never see his daughter again because he smoked crack. He smoked crack because he could never see his daughter again. I had nothing to offer him but platitudes and a sympathetic ear. All of this was pulling me off my mission. I had to find River, and Will was a distraction. Gripped with the hyperfocus of his stimulant high, Will needed my ear, my sympathy, my empathy. Will needed me to give him a hint as to why he should bother drawing another breath. I needed to find River. It was getting late, and I had work in the morning.

In a leap of faith, I took advantage of the fact that I'd been recognized to shed my camouflage and approach people more directly. I asked about the young woman, going as far as to feign recognition of people to build off an assumed rapport based on familiarity. It's not uncommon for parents and friends to canvas the streets seeking their loved ones. Establishing and maintaining trust was paramount. I discarded every scrap of my cop persona making sure it was heard that I was looking for a woman in order to help her. I made myself into a parent pleading for help from River's peers, someone comforting and safe, so that they could resume their lives without fear of arrest from undercover officers, or any other threat against which they were so vigilant.

That night the question murdered my sleep. I knew from past contacts with many of the people on both sides of that street that they had addresses in the same affluent suburbs of San Francisco like San Carlos and Burlingame. The police investigative part of my brain wanted to understand. The parent part of my brain needed to understand. Here I saw we are all potentially one back injury, car accident, sports injury, rape, night of partying, all night cramming session, new onset mental illness, or trauma of any kind away from a lifetime of addiction.

Many of the young people in the light would eventually lurk on the dark side of the street. None of us can know if we harbor a Hyde, lurking in the hardwiring in our brains, waiting for the crack formed by trauma or pain to emerge, its hands around the neck of Jekyll. Now it has been freed, and fight to keep him at bay must be maintained forever.

FINDING RIVER

D ays later, still searching for River, I found myself at the plaza once more. I had no idea what I was doing. I had no game plan, no experience or training to fall back on. As I breached the line of lost souls that bordered that vast gathering place where those on the night shift of the streets milled about, she saw me. She ran to me. Surprised, I stood unmoving, unsure if I would spook her, causing her to take flight. When she reached me, she threw her arms around me in a tight embrace, crying the emotional plea into my ear "I want to go home." She knocked me for a loop. Involvement in these people's lives was no longer a matter of choice for me.

My first encounter with River, she had been shooting up with a man I had assumed to be her boyfriend. The encounter was like most other I'd had with people taking drugs in the stations. There was an ugly confrontation, and I ended up arresting the man. Her only concern was for her companion's items. She asked if he would be going to jail. I was accustomed to this. On the street, women depend heavily on the men in romantic relationships for drugs and protection.

"Your boyfriend is going to be back; it won't be long—"

She cut me off and made it clear, "That's not my boyfriend. I just want to know what he wants me to do with his stuff."

This was also common. Any contraband he had on his person would likely be confiscated and added to his charges. Alternatively, if she took his belongings, she would have access to any drugs he still had.

The next time I saw her she was shooting up into her arm in the middle of a busy downtown station hallway in front of patrons and pedestrians in the early morning. I had recently avoided a physical fight with her companion and had kicked her out of the station. I was agitated at her insult to public decency and, after I confiscated her loaded syringe, berated her with stern language as I followed her down the hallway to the stairs. Turning her head over her left shoulder while dope-stumbling and slouching towards the stairs, she acknowledged my questions about what she was doing but did not lash out or return my tone like most did. She was hurting and would leave dope sick, wondering where and how to get her next hit. I had taken away her high, yet she was oddly compliant. She literally threw her hands up, sarcastically conceding her crime: "yeah, I'm shooting up, I'm a terrible person..."

I purposefully poked her for what would have been an understandably nasty response. I hoped the experience would keep her form coming back to shoot up, and that she might spread the word that BART was not a welcoming place for drug activity. Maybe they'd be more inclined to risk exposure in the alcoves of the iconic San Francisco architecture outside. My job was to ensure the safety of the halls. There was no policy and procedure on how to make drug addicts not come into the sanctity of the BART stations. It was all left to officer discretion.

A little over a month later, one week before River's 24th Christmas, I found her in the station in terrible shape. Before the police academy, I had been an Emergency Medical Technician. My last medical job was in the busy emergency department of the only level I trauma center in a 607 square mile county. I brought with me the experience of years of observing people in varying levels of physical distress. That part of me saw numerous red flags in River. I followed her as she stumbled as quickly as she could, falling forward with each step, gravity pulling her forward down a long corridor to the other side of the station as fast as her ailing body would allow.

Shook with the growing guilt of our previous encounter, I wanted desperately to try something new. I would apply the same lens through which I had viewed Miska. I would ignore the Substance Use Disorder and switch gears. I tried to reach out to her but at first, she didn't respond. Miserable and hurting, River did not want to talk. I recognized that she was in survival mode; a wounded animal seeking the safest place to hide and heal or disappear and die. I found myself panicking. This was my first true test. I didn't know what to do. I was sure that if I approached her in the wrong way, the stress would cause her to run off. I couldn't find the words, so I tapped into where my empathy was rooted: my role as a parent. I tried talking to her like I would my daughter, still she did not want to engage. She wanted to be left alone.

As I tried carefully to catch up to her, I saw her take me up on my offer to allow her to stay in the station. River clambered into a hidden bicycle rack storage area at the far end of the hallway. Slowly and quietly, I approached her. When I reached her, she was already unconscious on the floor, slouched against a bike rack and looking more like she had passed out than fallen asleep. I approached her in the partially walled off area and the overpowering stench of infection stopped me in my tracks. I hadn't smelled infection this strong even in the emergency department. She was clearly very sick, perhaps septic. River suffered a pallor I had only seen in corpses. I reverted to my EMT training that I slipped on as easily as a set of scrubs and assessed her. The medical term for my first observation is "pale and diaphoretic." I palpated her outstretched wrist and was shocked at how ice cold her arm was. I could find neither a radial nor brachial pulse. I felt for her carotid and found what I would have previously charted as a weak, thready, tachycardic, and slightly irregular pulse. No pulse in either limb is a sign of shock; her heart could not beat hard enough to create enough blood pressure to supply blood to her extremities. I was now concerned that she might be in, or close to the throes of potentially deadly septic shock.

I had seen a lot of sick people in the ED. I'd seen dying people, people who died while I and the rest of the medical staff furiously struggled to perform life saving measures. This was the first time I had seen a life shutting down in the field. I had no other techs, nurses, doctors, or medical equipment. I didn't even have my personal first aid kit or a beat partner.

I shook River awake and tried to talk to her like an EMT. She was furious at me for waking her, admonishing me to leave her. Part of me fought the reflex to give up on her, to say "fuck it, get out," calling for back up and moving her along. She was sprawled on a bicycle locker floor in a train station being told she needed to go to the hospital, with a cop desperately trying to shake her awake, and she did not care. She indignantly blurted she wanted to sleep and be left alone long enough to do so. I knew that if she slept now, she may never wake up.

As I so often found myself of late, I was in uncharted waters. I was desperate to formulate a safe plan for her. I considered my choices. If I called an ambulance, she would most likely either wander off before they arrived or refuse treatment when they did. I knew from experience that EMS cannot treat a patient without express consent. The only exceptions are in the case of unconsciousness and when a patient has been placed on a psychiatric hold, when consent is considered implied because a reasonable person in their right mind can be assumed to have consented if able to do so. I could call back up to assist me in removing her from the station. But I had already decided that was a dangerous option. Alone out there she was all but dead. Letting her sleep was as dangerous. I could wake her and let her go voluntarily, but she would still be alone. Before I could figure out the safest option, River bolted upright, managed to get to her feet, and power-stumbled towards the exit. I resisted an urge to grab her, the cop pushed aside by the EMT, the EMT restrained the cop. There was too much risk of harming her with physical restriction. The stress of a struggle could sap whatever chemicals were animating her. Her body did not know it, but she was a dead woman walking.

As she furiously cried at me to leave her alone, that she just wanted to rest, I blurted out an offer to come back and stay as long as she wanted. I pleaded, promising to leave her alone. It was too late. There was too much indignant momentum, and she was getting out of the station no matter what. The stairs were only a few yards away and she was closing the distance surprisingly rapidly. My mind reeled as I followed hopelessly behind her. I did not dare match her pace lest she feel she was being chased and crash on the stairs into a seizure, or quick death.

River reached the first half dozen steps as Galen approached me from behind, matching River's pace and passing me. I knew him well enough to have a rapport with him. Galen made eye contact with me as he passed by, acknowledging that he heard and saw what was going on. He said he would follow her and watch over her. I knew this to be true. Galen had a good heart and was liked in the homeless addict community. Galen was young and addicted himself. Just a week prior I had sent him to the hospital for a heroin overdose in the same location. While his Jekyll was sweet and well loved, Galen's Hyde had a death grip on him. He was deep in his own pit. That night he had just completed his fix to get him through the night and was returning to the station when he saw the commotion between River and me. Galen must have felt compelled to help her. Galen was a helper.

As River and Galen ascended the stairs in tandem, I sternly yelled out instructions to Galen: when her momentum wore off, she would collapse. When she did, he needed to call 911 as quickly as possible. She was likely going to die if there was any delay. Galen looked directly at me, and with reassuring confidence said he understood and would honor my request. She did collapse. He did make the call. Galen saved her life.

Later that week when my partner and I visited her on the hospital ward after her surgery, she told us with gratitude and humility that the doctors had removed a golf ball sized clot from against her jugular vein. The surgeons claimed they had never seen anyone survive such a malady in their entire medical careers. They also told her that if she continued hitting up, she would most definitely die. As we visited, I got my first taste of gratification from this work. I had done it. I had saved River. She would get healthy in the hospital and return home to her mother. I fixed her.

My wife was at Michael's, shopping with our daughter. Art was more therapeutic than anything else for her, and she greatly needed the fulfillment that came with it. They circled the aisles, looking for supplies for the newest of her fleeting interests: mosaics. River had loved writing from an early age. Since my wife shared that affinity, I asked for her help finding a suitable gift for River. A token of congratulations and encouragement to keep Hyde at bay and continue on her current path.

She listened as she rerouted from the ceramic tiles to the journals. Our daughter helped her pick out a nice pen. My wife knew something I didn't. Her mother had worked with at-risk young women. My wife knew that it was premature to call this a win, and that, while a noble effort, a journal and pen were gifts for much further on in her story. This purchase was for me, not for River.

Two weeks after I returned with her gift, River eloped from the hospital.

I was furious with her. I was furious with myself. I had wanted that win so badly, I had made it about me, not River. I thought she was cured. I was riding that high, and she dared take that from me. I wasn't meeting her where she was, I hadn't yet climbed into the pit with her. I was realizing that in that role as a helper, connecting to my empathy meant having responsibility for a deeper insight into myself. I had to separate the gratification I got from helping people from being on their level, but I didn't yet know how. It would take constant self-reflection to avoid the temptation to help others purely to chase that high.

On another set of after shift rounds in the square, River approached me and asked me for help. I needed to save her. I called my wife again. I told her I'd found River, that I couldn't just leave her out there. That I wanted to bring her home. She fell silent. Her mother had brought women home in an effort to save them. That never ended well. Hearing her hesitation, I quickly added that of course we didn't have room in the house, but we lived on a large property at the base of Mount Diablo. It was warm out, and we had camping equipment. A tent and an air mattress between the chickens and the cows on the peaceful mountainside was surely better than the streets with the thieves and rapists. She knew better. But because she did, she agreed.

River told me she'd think about it. Of course, our piece of land was far from rapists, but it was also far from access to drugs. River was still addicted, and for someone with Substance Use Disorder, drugs move up on Maslow's Hierarchy of Needs above shelter and food. River could also see that I genuinely cared about her and was doing everything I could think of to help her. She was not about to disrespect that. Not while Jekyll was here. Her noncommittal answer was her gift of hope to me.

I lost track of her again. But because she made herself the focus of my empathy, the cop in me lost out to the parent and I became desperate. This desperation motivated me to build the tools I initially employed in the single-minded task of saving River, but that would continue to serve me in the shadows of the Graham Theatre. The most important of these tools were the people I brought into the fold. The helpers. I recruited people like Galen, those who had a natural affinity for looking out for their own. Will, who so desperately clutched his crack pipe that night by the UN Plaza, would become my single most valuable partner on the streets. I wonder if I could determine how many people Will helped save from that life, as he perpetually struggled, trapped in his own cycle of shame and guilt, never able to escape himself.

I gifted my helpers with the ineffable feeling of satisfaction evoked by altruism, and they accepted gladly. Sharing with them my wins, I built a team that became a community with me at the center. I was their source of harm reduction whether it was in the form of allowing them to make a phone call on my work cell, passing messages to their families, mail from families to them, or simply telling them the time of day: a connection to social norms that is important to the homeless.

I learned how their community worked, the nuts and bolts of life on the street. I realized this was the only way to be efficient in this work. I figured out how to meet them where they were. Over time I became an accepted presence on and off duty, allowed into their urban wilderness. My helpers began to observe on my behalf. They watched and reported back, giving me information about River's habits and last known whereabouts.

The deeper into this work I dove, the more I came home with emotional conundrums. I asked about altruism, about self-serving generosity. I spoke about my distress at the feeling that there was no true selflessness, because giving always brought pleasure to the giver. My wife waxed philosophical, finally surrendering and relenting that the absence of true selflessness was outweighed by the gains of the benefactors. That wasn't helpful.

My team of volunteers and I kept at it, though, and communicating with her parents, were able to get her location to her father. He met her where she was, visiting her regularly and spending time with her in her tent. Not long after I got the call: she was home. Later Galen fell to his demons, the only son of an African immigrant mother who watched him slowly die.

ERIC HOFSTEIN

JOSEPH

I realized I was surveying a mass casualty scene with the sick, wounded, traumatized, whose bodies pumped blood and oxygen but offered little executive function, their experiences devoid of everything but the need to satisfy the cravings of the limbic system. They were disheveled, partially or fully naked, with months or years of filth cemented into their skin. The parasites including bedbugs, fleas, and lice, were so healthy and fat that you could see them from a distance as an undulating mass. Exposed skin was pocked with the telltale reddish pink circles caused by ringworm and bumps from scabies that come from sleeping in the dirt. The more serious cases walked about with peeled flaps of flesh so thick and deep muscle was exposed beneath and ravaged by antibiotic resistant infections Methicillin-resistant Staphylococcus aureus (MRSA) and Vancomycin-resistant Staphylococcus aureus (VRSA).

I watched them collecting and hoarding odd items and fighting with ghosts only they knew. Having rebuffed reality, they were trapped in the purgatory of their own mind.

Officers get to know the dispossessed and their inherent quirks: muttered phrases on repeat, specific items they always carried around, and distinct physical mannerisms all so typical of the individual so that an officer could easily recognize them from these sorts of details the dispatchers gave. There was one who had a "thing" for fire extinguishers. Any time he saw one, he'd break through the glass and carry it around. He never used them; he just liked to ride the trains with one in hand, then replace it with a new one when it presented itself. Officers always knew he was around when the maintenance crew complained about missing fire extinguishers on train cars and in the stations, or if officers found one sitting upright in the middle of a train platform.

Commonly it was necessary to drive from one San Francisco station to another, when the trains were stopped or delayed due to obstacles or people on the tracks or on weekends when there were fewer trains and officers had to get from station to station quicker than train travel would allow. On many of these occasions, my partner and I witnessed still more disparate lives lived by the marginalized. One night we watched as a gentleman, gave a competition-worthy rhythmic gymnastics routine, using yellow caution tape as his ribbons, in the nude, down the middle of San Francisco's major thoroughfare of Market Street, for several blocks. Another night my partner, a rookie, peered out the window at a man who lay motionless on the sidewalk and learned this lesson.

"Is he—dead?" he asked.

"I don't know, let's find out." It's not clear the

exact point I started talking like a grizzled old cop from an 80s action film, but I had my partner pull over the cruiser, a quick primary assessment showed the man was on death's doorstep. I pulled out my department issued Narcan, and with the conditioning afforded by repeated use, I deftly placed the nozzle into the nostril and dosed the still body.

The form bolted upright. I inquired of the body, "You want an ambulance?"

"No!" he replied, abruptly jumping to his feet and running into the distance with a speed and agility that surprised us both.

"No," I finished, "he isn't dead."

Unfortunately, a few days later we saw another man under the same circumstances. This was not unusual. This time, as the body lay in rigor mortis on the asphalt of one of the most celebrated cities on earth, instead of EMS waiting with him in dignity, alongside him was parked the same flatbed pickup trucks that collect roadkill. I never confirmed that it was the same person I'd Narcan'd before. My new partner was initially eager to learn about outreach, but by the time I retired, I didn't think he would apply to the newly formed outreach unit.

On rare occasions I would see one of the displaced in a temporary reprieve from their mental purgatory, so I would speak with their long lost and deeply buried Jekyll, who somehow still clung to life inside the shared mind. One young man, Joseph, even told me in a moment of medicated clarity that when he was in his usual chaotic

Hyde state, I should be careful with him because he "will eat the paint off the walls."

When I first met Joseph curled up in a corner of a BART station corridor, he was very young in his early twenties. A little bit over five feet tall and slight of stature he gave the appearance of being delicate and easily breakable. I learned that Joseph's mother was a heavy drug user when pregnant with him and was long dead from a drug overdose. His father was in a Single Resident Occupancy and couldn't bring his son inside because it would violate the strict rules of a city funded SRO. He was young, alone, homeless, and almost always possessed by his Hyde, infected by a disease he had no hand in contracting, the effects over which he had no control. Inflicted in vitro with his mother's disorder, he never had a chance.

In that one moment of clarity, I was able to briefly speak to him, his Jekyll. During the conversation I determined he still had the remnants of the powerful antipsychotics coursing through him from a recent mental health commitment. I could see however, that when the drugs eventually burned out of Joseph's system he would go back to his assumed state, his Hyde waiting patiently as the short-lived effects of the antipsychotics waned and Jekyll slowly dragged back to a personal hell. Joseph was engaging when he was in that clear state of mind. He was friendly and we talked about many things. But when he slipped back into Hyde, he was easily angered and had an obsessive habit of popping the fat parasites he plucked from his groin hairs and laying them out in patterned displays in the middle of the BART hallway floors causing commuters to call 911 for a welfare check or to complain of him exposing himself.

I saw many *Josephs* in the city, day, and night. I could hear them wildly hollering while breaking things. They left behind detritus so common that employees of BART and adjacent business alike shared the morning routine of cleaning what one officer termed "BART diamonds": glass shards that the wanderers had smashed the night before; broken locks and discarded items that had not been worth stealing for drug money. I saw them meandering the streets oblivious to the cars around them. They needed steady doses of powerful medications to keep them safe, but without being compelled by a 5150, there is no way of getting people in mental health crises the help they need. Even so, as often as not they are immediately released when presented to the doctors, or heavily dosed with powerful medications until they comply and are discharged back to their own devices.

About a year after I met Joseph, I began working with outreach workers trying to figure out a plan to help him. Although there were many like him in the halls, he was getting heightened attention due to the involvement of a regular BART commuter of significant status and wealth wielding his power like a weapon against an unarmed foe. He filmed Joseph making his parasite displays and lying on the floors, sending the images with angry texts directly to the BART Police Department chief and BART board of directors. It was obvious to me and the outreach workers upon reading the forwarded messages that he was someone who equally detested the word 'no'.

I did not have much time to spare in this work, it was all voluntary and took place between 911 calls.

The BART system averaged 450,000 riders daily on weekdays alone. These riders were encouraged to employ an app to anonymously report incidents they witnessed. These incidents could be 'phone snatches' which were coordinated efforts, usually three-man teams, who would case train cars to narrow down individual victims and communicating silently snatch the smart phones from the victim's hand mid-scroll, exiting the train with practiced timing. A rider could report on the app, it would go to dispatch who would then dispatch officers at the station where the suspects exited or the next station the train was headed to, as the trains are tracked in real time. The officer at the next station could do a train sweep, locating the suspect, if possible, interview witnesses and investigate the crime. Or perhaps someone used foul language, stood too close, or otherwise offended someone on a train car stuffed full of one hundred or more tired, cranky, passengers, thick with the breath and body odor of a full day's work and it was just too much to bear, someone must get this person off this train. Pull out the phone, open the app. Report.

I was constantly pulled away from phone calls with emotionally wrought families, meetings with case workers or other allies, research to find resources and families, and helping those who came to me seeking help and resources. I may not ever have a window to reach out to the elusive community of homeless because someone on a crowded train car looked at someone else funny, and I had to investigate whether the passenger had nefarious intentions or perhaps was just socially awkward. It was an unnecessary distraction from prioritizing the needs for those in dire straits. My priorities were not my own.

Per protocol, I was expected to get Joseph up off the floor, perhaps offer him a pamphlet. I could go as far as calling a case worker if so inclined. In this case, however, the onus was on me because I knew Joseph. I felt an obligation to do more than push him out of the station and resolve BART's issue with him. This would require a lot of manhours. I had to find and gather resources and find allies in the system who were willing to work as hard for Joseph as I was. I had to plead Joseph's case, one in the 8,000 homeless on the San Francisco streets fighting for the crumbs offered by the various outreach agencies at play. I had to make phone calls, write emails, and gather information on Joseph's behalf when the two two-officer teams didn't have time for meal breaks. My beat partners were already taking on extra work to allow for my outreach. I resorted to making calls while walking through the stations to my dispatched calls as patrons complained that an officer was on personal calls on duty. I was subjected to an Internal Affairs investigation over just such a complaint. I literally risked my career trying to help a family save their child, sibling, parent, from the cold, damp, fog-shrouded streets, outside the purview of my law enforcement duties.

For over a year the texts came in and the caseworkers and I struggled to help Joseph find ways to connect to case workers to give him his meds. It was the same vicious cycle: each time Joseph would be in a hospital getting the meds he needed. Upon release, his case worker would be alerted. I would try to connect with that city case worker to help him find Joseph in the BART stations since Joseph was a creature of habit. The case worker would sometimes connect and then try to keep Joseph on a steady routine of getting his medications.

Surprisingly, Joseph was happily compliant at first, and I even saw him a few more times in moments of medicated clarity as he would go to the clinic from BART to get his medications after his early morning routines. But every time he got stable, he would slip back into the abyss until eventually he would reach the point of instability that caused him to lose enough awareness to know to go to the clinic. My sightings and coordination with the case worker were sporadic which made them ineffectual, and Joseph would spiral back into chaos until his next compelled hospital stay.

And so it went, the offended affluent texting, case worker only able to do so much, and Joseph abusing his body and mind until one day, he disappeared, and I never saw him again. For a while, I held out hope that he got into housing with follow up care or a clinic, but none of the case workers I spoke to could find Joseph. More than likely, he died, like many others in his situation.

PROOF OF LIFE

I t was deep into winter after the holidays, that time of year when there is nothing to look forward to but more wet cold and the eventuality of a spring still months away. This seasonal dead zone is the most dangerous time of year for the homeless: the rainy season in California. Common colds and the flu are at their height this theme of year, attacking weakened immune systems that are bombarded by the elements. Poorly clothed bodies that have been wracked by lack of a proper diet are already infected from dirty, diseased syringes. They languish, vulnerable and predisposed to the ravages of disease. It didn't take much for sickness to rapidly spread through the homeless community, adding an extra layer of fear for families praying for the survival of their loved ones. Sickness and misery are strong motivators for any modicum of change when one is miserable enough, and requests for housing always increase around this time which complicates outreach efforts. My cases grew exponentially as I contacted masses of homeless passed out on floors and trains seeking warm dry refuge.

Ten people turned to thirty, thirty to sixty, sixty

to 100 and more as I triaged homeless addicts and mentally ill subjects into my list of cases, connecting me to over two dozen families. I functioned as their conduit, the physical embodiment of a message and mail center, operating as a sort of street therapist for both family and addict as I helped them reconnect to lost support systems. Using the tools I gained resolving family disputes in patrol over the years and the knowledge I gleaned from reading literature, I eked out methods for Helping families and homeless loved ones reconnect. However, with success the added caseloads of messages and information sharing grew. Family love letters, care packages, and other items would be mailed to me and shoved into my small officer cubby in the lineup room by confused uniformed civilians. Tethers to their Jekyll's past and in turn Jekyll's tether to the loved ones who held out hope he would one day return to them. Families who may have pushed too hard in the past with demands of change and sobriety, now settled for the simplicity of proof life.

I saw the effect of mail and pictures families emailed or texted for me to share with homeless loved ones. It gave me an idea for how to dig deeper into their lost humanity no matter how deep it dwelled beneath the ferocity of Hyde's grip. I downloaded and printed the photos, then sealed them in opaque plastic evidence envelopes to protect them from the elements. I then slipped them into my vest carrier to hand out when I found the family member they were for. Sometimes the delivery was made as they were wandering around in a narcotic induced haze, sometimes on the way to make drug purchase, sometimes passed out; in which case I'd leave the package for them or give it to a friend to deliver when they regained consciousness. It always triggered a strong reaction and timid 'thank you's, sometimes from a downward turned gaze as if they were too embarrassed make eye contact.

The most satisfying deliveries for me were to the homeless who were doing what the inmates call *eating time.* Existing in time more than living life; waiting for something to change by happenstance, luck, or lack thereof; pondering and pontificating on why and how they got where they were. They got so excited at getting something completely unexpected and deeply important to their humanity, packaged materials from family, they would rip them open like a kid on Christmas morning. I would watch them with the satisfaction of a parent as they stared at the contents then carefully replace them into the plastic envelopes to carry around or place in their tent to stare at later. Pictures were a strong hook for Jekyll who would always bubble to the surface to peek at images of the past and present life from which they were isolated living inside the impenetrable bell jar. They expected nothing from life beyond the suffering and misery that were inherent conditions of a life of addiction and homelessness. To receive anything that touched on their humanity spoke directly to Jekyll and was as emotionally uplifting as it was unexpected.

If they were motivated enough to cast aside their shame and guilt enough to reconnect with the loved ones who sent me the pictures, I would offer to let them use my work phone if time allowed. If they did want to connect but were too scared or embarrassed to make the phone call themselves, I'd offer to make the call for them and pass on a message, advocating on their behalf and handle the emotionally difficult first contact. If that was too difficult, I would offer to craft and text a message for them. It was a two-way street, and I would ask them for permission to send a current photo to the families, some who had not seen them in years, in one case more than fourteen years. As I advocated and mediated both sides, they always reciprocated by sharing personal stories weaving verbalized historical tapestries of lives before and after Hyde emerged.

My goal was to help the families comprehend what life for their drug addicted homeless loved one looked like, what was enabling and what was helping someone who is addicted and homeless. The toughest and most common questions I was asked were 'I know I shouldn't send cash but they once called from jail/streets/hospital and said they were hungry so I did' or 'They want their stimulus check, it's their money'; or 'Can I send them socks' or 'Can I send you a backpack?' It was common for them to ask for backpacks and say their phone was stolen.

I educated these families and support systems so they could have realistic conversations and to relieve fears and trepidations. I explained how city services worked and where free food was delivered daily. I told them where clothing could be obtained from churches and resource centers. This way, they knew what was available and what wasn't when they received requests of emergency relief. They could consider these things and whether the call was from Jekyll or Hyde.

I helped families to view the duality of a sufferer of substance use and mental health disordered personality. I found there was a pervasive aura of angry disappointment from trust violated many times over.

Viewing their loved one in the context of a duality seemed to bring an emotional release and understanding, a compassion and empathy they had formerly not allowed themselves to feel, or had been afraid to, lest their trust be violated again due to more false promises, lies, and deceitful behavior

That separation of identity helps to compartmentalize emotions and separate love from hate. They can feel hate, they can feel love, and logically justify the separation of feelings, love, rage, regret, loss, separated into what I have named Jekyll and Hyde. I explained Hyde's domination of Jekyll and that the longer Hyde is present, the stronger and more dominant he becomes. Narcotics (or whatever the subject of addiction, I'll use narcotics for illustration here,) are a crutch, a defense against pain. The balance of dosage versus relief is where the danger lurks. Narcotics release and feed Hyde. The effects have an exponential impact on daily life. There can be long periods of what appear to be equanimity followed by a sudden crash into relapse, chaos, and even violence. There is a slow build under the surface that those afflicted with Substance Use Disorder and those suffering from mental health issues become adept at masking from even the closest of friends and relatives. Like a method actor, they are convincing because they believe it themselves, to their own detriment.

The first phone calls to family were full of elation and hope, psychological release from the worst aspect of losing a loved one to the streets and addiction, not knowing. I told them about the guilt and shame cycle and because of that I recommended not connecting by phone call as the first contact. I recommended that they build slowly with messaging via an intermediary (me) or a more neutral family member. When I spoke with the person who was on the street, disconnected, I advised that person that when picking a point of contact to keep connected to, they should pick the family member they felt most comfortable with. I helped them prepare mentally and emotionally by getting any triggering questions out of the way before making contact with me. That may look like a family asking why they couldn't send a message that they were at least alive. A common answer I'd explain is the loss of time mentally due to the bell jar affect.

As I worked with the homeless, I noticed a pattern: the longer time between contacts with family, the more difficult any contact will be. The more emotional and embarrassing, and a feel for need to explain the long absence. Emotions are painful, and an addict is extremely sensitive to pain, it makes them want to use which then compounds the issue. I commonly saw homeless addicts feel tremendous guilt and self-hatred for hurting their families, and continually hurting their families with their worrying and concern. Their philosophy becomes *I'd rather they mourn me than pine for me.* The longer the gap between contact, the more likely they are to give in to this belief and cut themselves off for good.

ERIC HOFSTEIN

WORK TO BE DONE

One bittersweet win illustrates well why I do this work: during a check of the Civic Center station my beat partner and I found one of the young women we were working with who was homeless and heavily addicted to opiates. She was curled up on hallway floor wet and shivering after stumbling inside the station during a rainstorm. Wearing only a T shirt and jeans, she could barely talk she was so hypothermic. It was a quiet moment during our shift, so we warmed her up in a patrol car parked above the station and then took her to a Salvation Army center and bought her some dry clothes and a winter jacket because there was no repository for the thousands of homeless to go to in a moment of need. I realized that this could happen again to any one of the homeless yet for all of the millions of dollars spent on services and resources they only operated Monday to Friday, 9:00 am to 5:00 pm, no matter how much we complained about it. It was the single biggest hurdle in doing any outreach work. If an addict was ready for rehab, needed to contact a case worker, wanted to connect to a resource in a time of need, they were out of luck on weekends, holidays, and at night. The police were the only professional agency assisting people that was out in the public to help others twenty-four hours a day, seven days a week without exception.

Cell phones, charger cords, charging stations, ponchos, socks, underwear, and emergency blankets were the most desired items, but I also realized that they didn't have the luxury of a safe place to keep their things. Free locker facilities were rife with criminal activity and difficult to access for a homeless person. IDs, backpacks, phones, and even the shoes on their feet were stolen daily. I was learning what daily life was truly like through their eyes. I could feel their needs and wants living on the streets, addicted, mired in mental health disorders. I helped them learn where to get what they called "Obama phones" phones available through federal funds through the Lifeline Assistance Program (well before President Obama's administration,) city ID cards including booking photos that the city had a policy of accepting as legitimate ID for city services. I had parents mail out photocopies of ID cards and paperwork. Some sent me care packages with envelopes stuffed full of letters from friends and families.

I gathered some donated emergency supplies from a city program I worked with and kept them in boxes and cabinets in various areas of our tiny precinct rooms. My coworkers and other employees who used the precinct saw what I was doing and a short time later I came into work to find replenished supplies, donated clothes from their families, and even some of the station agents had pitched in. We became a community helping a community in need because there was nowhere else to go. The downside was that it is a small precinct with extremely limited space, and some of my peers were not exactly comfortable with my donation center sprinkled about the office.

The upside to this arrangement was my amusement at watching very masculine tactical type male officers, some who were former military, pop open a cabinet looking for work supplies only to pull out feminine hygiene products and underwear with a delicate two finger grasp. I'd follow the very confused expressions waiting for the right moment to announce "That's mine. Don't worry, they're unused...I think." Sadly, I was unaware when I first stocked up from the program that donated supplies why they had so many feminine hygiene products available: women stop having their menses living on the streets. It was a stark reminder of how damaging life on the streets can be to even the youngest and healthiest people.

Knowing the people I worked with had no way to keep them safe, I offered to hold on to important items like ID cards and hand them photocopies when their property was stolen. Some took me up on this offer and I would get the occasional knock on the precinct door from someone who needed a copy of their paperwork or ID. Although they almost always appeared to be in a hurry, they'd request to look through the donated clothing. It was a bit uncomfortable for the work environment, as they'd block a hallway or office with working cops as odiferous 'transients' rifled through clothing. I was worried someone would complain and I would have to suspend my efforts, so I felt I had to hurry them along and keep these contacts short. That was counterintuitive to maintaining my rapport building and harm reduction work with them. This gave rise to the idea of forming my own non-profit that would allow me to continue the work the way I felt it should be done.

My career seemed to be pulling me along some sort of dreadful timeline of the corruption of children. I was trapped witnessing an inescapable cycle of innocence, wounded and gnarled by the trauma of life into the ghosts we turn a blind eye to on our city streets.

When I was on street patrol before BART, I used to get dispatched to family disturbances, restraining order violations, where the elderly parents of now an adult child would call 911 not knowing what else to do. Their child lost to drugs and crime, mental illness and homelessness showed up and tried to break in. In a drunken, drugged out, or mental illness fueled tirade went back to the place of comfort and sanctuary, the homes and family of their days before the monster got them tossed out or alienated from. They'd pound on the doors, open windows, argue, plead, and threaten the elderly occupants with indignant rage that it was their home too, and to let them in.

Sometimes these acts were in violation of a court stay away order from a criminal case where they had battered their elderly parent and committed elder abuse. Sometimes it was in violation of a valid protection order previously served as a last-ditch attempt suggested by some random officer for a prior incident of threats and violence. The pain of a parent who once held their baby and fed and nurtured the child, protecting the child, now seeking court protection from that same child is soul crushing. I witnessed it hundreds of times, yet even now I cannot express it in words.

As the list of the lost children with whom I worked grew, I reached a point where I finally understood why elderly parents so often stopped time in their homes, leaving their children's rooms in mint condition like a mausoleum faithfully waiting for the return of a long dead child that would never return. I walked into these time capsules morbidly curious. Photographs from baseball practice, trophies, movie posters, stuffed animals that held nightmares at bay all silently waited for a child who would never return. Listening to the stories about what the adult had done, I faithfully jotted notes for my police report. Now they sent me pictures of the lost lives. Years later, sitting in line up at BART while briefing was held, I'd scroll though the newest photos glancing at key words in the accompanying texts, infant pictures, sibling group photos, family outings with joyful beams. My mind flooded with emotion with every picture.

I'd glance between the current photos I took posted on the poster board my peers made for me attached to my self-made BOLOs (Be On the Look Out) of those lost Jekyll-children now trapped in adult bodies with their Hydes. "Hofstein's Hotline" they semi-sarcastically labeled my poster board. And on that poster board names and images went up and down as my work grew; some saved, some lost, but some always remained, until my last day when I had to take down my work to go into retirement: one remains. And so remains, the work to be done.

In line up before my first call for service I turned on my phone. In flooded the texts and the emotions; the pain of a family's loss painted with family photos from crib to high school. Pictures of family moments illustrated a family's desperation to punctuate the depths of their loss.

Those pictures chipped away at my defenses and pulled me deep into the pit with those families. They became my family photos, and I became fixated on the hunt for their (my?) children. Sometimes it felt like they were trying to prove to me, as if I was a morality court officer, that Jekyll did indeed exist. They wanted me to advocate to any resources or agencies what a person of value their loved one was. They wanted me to understand that finding and confronting Hyde running the streets of San Francisco was an imperative; a kidnapping case. Hyde had absconded with Jekyll. "I want my beautiful child back!" "Please find my child! Hyde kidnapped and abuses them! I just want to hear their voice again!"

I was primed with a sense of panic and urgency that my beat partners felt and it irritated them. The early morning hours were when many homeless people were collapsed in stairwells and BART entrance alcoves seeking safety and the warm dry air of the stations to pass out in after their drug use and nightly wanderings in the cold city nights. Our sweeps were the first order of business and my best opportunities for finding the homeless addicts I with whom I sought contact.

In the cold winter months I loaded up my cargo pockets with emergency camping ponchos and emergency thermal mylar blankets that look like massive sheets of aluminum foil. I would make my morning rounds, sweeps at the entrances of the stations and sometimes at the library across the street where I'd find people in various stages of hypothermia with little clothing to protect them from the elements. Once I found an elderly woman who was recently evicted and slowly freezing to death in the public library doorway.

So lost and confused she was, she did not know about the city shelters or who to call. She simply saw a public building and curled up with her suitcase and thin layer of clothing and silently slipped into hypothermia. I became known for having the emergency blankets and homeless would sometimes approach me to ask for a blanket, and especially the ponchos. I had fewer of them but they were an especially sought-after item. I learned how bad the thieving was when I noticed one winter many homeless walking around barefoot. Some of them extremely upset and lashing out or crying, cold, and miserable. Around that time I noticed a lot of them were sleeping barefoot with their shoes under their slumbering heads. I asked some of them why they did this, exposing their feet to the frigid night air and using a shoe like a pillow. I was told that thefts were getting so bad that the shoes were stolen off their feet while they slept. That led to a cascade affect where shoes went up in value in the homeless population like any suddenly hot item in any market. Not much different than the lines of humanity that would snake thought parking lots of stores waiting for toilet paper purchase during the COVID years.

This was the work. I developed a methodology, yes, but it was the people who drove me. It was they who taught me. I listened, to them, I saw them, and I learned from them. It was not the professionals with the years of studies and degrees who taught me how to empathize and reduce harm and improve lives. It was the people who lived it.

ERIC HOFSTEIN

GUY WALKS INTO A BAR

A general invite goes out to everyone's email an hour before the workday ends. All are invited to gather at one of the nicer bar and grills for drinks and food. Some can make it for a little socialization, others have family responsibilities to rush off to as soon as they punch out. You decide spending a little time with peers before you go home won't complicate your life. After finishing off a little preparation work to ease responsibilities for the next day's shift you freshen up and make yourself as presentable as a workplace bathroom will allow and head out the door to carpool with a couple of others.

On the short drive everyone takes a turn joking about bosses and ambitious coworker goofs with strange quirks, conversations saved for off work hours. Socializing with peers who share in the stress and anxiety of daily life together offers each one a turn to prove themselves a member of the tribe rather than an outlier to be distrusted when they all let their hair down.

At the venue, an overworked waitress escorts the group to the party sized tables. As you approach you notice a particular coworker has beat everyone else there and is working on what appears to be a half empty drink, soon to partner with the empty glass that hasn't even been sitting long enough to leave a mark on the table. It's happy hour and he wants to take advantage of every minute. His name, often spoken in hushed tones at work, is answered now with loud greetings. Too loud: he's already feeling the effects of his head start and his giddiness is more a relief from craving than true mirth at seeing his peers. His closest relationships come out of bottles rather than from people. He is always first in, last out, and quickest to finish each drink. Everyone notices but no one has a close enough relationship to have the most important conversation with him, instead passing the days in silent consensus that if his work performance is affected, then that is a responsibility for supervisors to address.

Time passes more easily than expected. Happy hour is gone but he's still going strong, flowing with a momentum only an experienced liver could handle. You know the pattern well, the next day he will be late or bang out "sick" and you wonder if he can have any Paid Time Off left on the books. You feel enough sympathy to try and intervene enough to broach the subject, but don't dare make that a reality. You appropriately assume denial and a quick change of subject will be the response, an acknowledgement of "I got a problem" and "it's affecting my work and life" are not foreseeable outcomes. He's smart enough to get where he has in life, he must be smart enough to see what is obvious to everyone else: he drinks too much and it affects his job. More than a heads-up warning on something so deeply personal is the responsibility of a supervisor or spouse.

The next day as predicted it's fifteen minutes into the shift and his desk is empty with his office lights still off. You know traffic will be the excuse but not the fact behind his eventual late arrival. You still feel sympathy, but only so much, because you and everyone else are responsible enough to handle your lives well enough to keep a job, pay the bills, maintain a family. Still, your conscience gets the best of you and you make a quiet call in a back room on your personal phone to give him his wake-up call. He answers and the stress in his tone is palpable. An impossibly short time later he rushes in, making a beeline to the boss's office, visibly mouthing what you assume is a practiced speech of excuses. The boss waves him in and in that moment, you don't know if you will look away or watch the interaction. Perhaps the boss is going to finally fire him or suspend him. This time maybe just chew him out. You may feel a primal glee, glad that poor schlub is the three-legged antelope in the office herd, and not you, his detriment a *'better him than me'* sense of relief. Maybe you could have saved him from this. Maybe a conversation the night before would have prevented this.

Consider whether your opinion of him as a person and his situation change if you knew he had a genetic predisposition for alcoholism and he had crippling clinical depression and an anxiety disorder not completely treatable by medications.

Now think of this: he gets fired, and about a year later you and your coworkers meet up after work for food and drinks and as you walk to the front door, you see him. Slumped over on the sidewalk disheveled, gaunt, filthy and odoriferous, obviously intoxicated, he tries to engage with pedestrians to ask for money. Ask yourself if you engage with him or shy away with guilt and embarrassment. Really ponder if you would feel different about your thoughts and actions - or lack thereof - that night and morning after when you could have tried to connect with him about his drinking?

Homelessness and addiction are not an identity or personality type, the same way we wouldn't tell someone they act like a cancer patient. It is a condition, a result of a set life circumstances and events, mental health conditions, and even genetics. When I say addict what image comes to mind and do you make assumptions about why they're an addict?

No two addicted people are the same, no two homeless people are the same, not even if they were identical twins. Panoptic labels create common, subjective tropes that worm their way into the social consciousness as "common knowledge." Overly simplistic views tailor policies and procedures and become sociopolitical agendas, tainted by confirmation bias rooted in emotions rather than objectivity. In reality, it is impossible to feel true empathy if we can't *feel* where another person is on their emotional spectrum. Our need to rationalize the behaviors of an addict is bogged down in the confusion between ascribing rational thought to irrational behavior and is a common place where relationships with addicts fall into disarray. I discovered that striving to understand the emotional component to actions and not seeking the rational thoughts behind behaviors, was the key to understanding the homeless, those who are in pain and misery.

How addiction happens, whether there are common reasons for homelessness and addiction, these are the questions that drove me deep into their world. I wanted to understand and find resolutions, but I found academics and academia sterile and too clinical for the reality of the real-life tapestries that littered the darkest places civilized society has to offer. I looked at Maslow's Hierarchy of needs and discovered that to build a conceptual framework of needs to apply to the harm reduction model, I needed to look at each person as a product of a unique set of circumstances that will change moment to moment. The alcoholic in a bar during happy hour will be less likely to be motivated for positive change than he will the next morning waking up late for work, facing professional and personal repercussions.

I would have to be flexible and open minded. The human brain filters information through the emotional filter before the prefrontal cortex gets involved so our emotions lead our prioritization of needs. They control our actions on a rudimentary level and often control higher functions which makes them a window to the truth of our motivations.

I tried to find relevant information in the sciences to academically explain some of my observations. I looked at how Maslow described blocks of a pyramid that set a hierarchy of needs. It made sense for some people, the neurotypical. But in the world of homelessness and addiction, mental health disorders and brain altering narcotics cause atypical, neurodivergent, behaviors that don't fit any standardized predictable reactions to stimuli.

When someone falls out of society and is emotionally, mentally, and physically traumatized, perhaps pumped full neurobiological altering chemicals, that pyramid gets deconstructed and reconstructed like a Rubik's Cube from moment to moment. The more time that passes in this life the more profound and impactful the effects on their physiology and psychology. What you think is a priority or need for them based on what feels like 'common sense' may be completely wrong.

I discovered this lesson when I worked with a young homeless woman. She was smart, very witty with a sardonic sense of humor. Her body degraded while her mind remained intact, and she had tremendous empathy for others around her. She was usually more concerned for her peers than herself, as long as she got her fix. She had fallen out of life in an affluent East Bay community on to the streets of San Francisco. Homeless and heavily addicted to opiates, her medication for a chaotic childhood in an abusive family environment made her immune to any benefits of wealth and means. She chose homelessness over life with her dysfunctional family and traumatizing home environment. Every day I came to work I checked the navigation centers and shelters looking for a bed to become available and hoped I would be able to find her when one did. It became a mission, a priority.

One shift as I made my rounds, I saw she was hanging out at the Civic Center and when I contacted her, she told me she would be there all day. Towards the end of my shift, I called the shelters and residency programs and sure enough, a bed at a much-requested brand new navigation facility was available. I watched the clock and when the shift ended I dressed down quickly to get to her before the opportunity was lost. As I rushed up the escalator I found her sitting in the streetlamp lit plaza. It was extremely cold out and she was hunched over in clothing inappropriate for the frigid night to come. Of all nights to save her, it was on this night that would most assuredly claim the lives of some of her peers. Giddy with excitement, I announced the good news to her as soon as I got within earshot. With emotional flatness she averted her gaze as I stood in front of her. She looked down, avoiding any direct eye contact as she appeared to be trying to form the words to respond to me.

Only one short sentence came out, "I'm waiting for someone."

I was incensed, hurt. *Waiting for someone!* I struggled for months to get her resources after she insisted that she wanted help from me and was ready to make changes. I helped her on my personal time, and finally succeeded at getting her a bed on one of the coldest nights of the year. It felt personal, like she had lied to me, jerked me around when I worked so hard to help her. I wanted to lash out and hurt her feelings, then walk away from her for good as a lesson. I felt what so many others felt when lied to or manipulated by an addict: they want something, plead for something, make promises, then let you down. My feelings must have been obvious in my reaction because she seemed to notice.

As I was seething in emotional confusion, she glanced up at me, and in a subdued voice thanked me and looked away again, returning to her silence.

I'm still unsure why, maybe it was the lessons I

learned from Juana and other connections I made, but I realized something: "You're waiting for someone who is bringing you your next hit."

Without hesitation she glanced at me making eye contact and quietly muttered, "yes."

As a deputy this response would have reinforced my negative feelings about her intentions. But now that I had a deeper understanding of homelessness and addiction, I saw her differently. To admit to a cop, to turn down my help, saw her sincerity. There were many ways she could have lied to me. She could have said she was starving and waiting for food, and I would have believed her. This was a raw self-shaming confession like she was sitting at confessional bearing her deepest thoughts.

This sits with me and informs how I help others. I assumed her priority was shelter, as she confirmed in many previous contacts. In that moment, in the freezing cold windy night of San Francisco, her priority on her pyramid of needs was not shelter, or safety, or even comfort of warmth and a bed. It was her street medication. That taught me a lesson in the power of addiction and self-medicating with narcotics.

My initial feelings were selfish and subjective. I evaluated her physiological and psychological needs through my own, feeling the bite of the cold winter night thinking she was hunched over from the cold. She wasn't. She was getting dope sick, her internal pain outmatching any external discomfort from the cold so I assumed I was looking at the bottom of her abyss, but I was not. And in my obvious disappointment she felt empathy for me and my emotional pain bringing more shame on herself telling me what she had to know would disappoint me and fly in the face of all the work I had done to help her. Even in the depths of her encroaching dope sick misery she showed more empathy towards me than I had towards her.

She knew what I was feeling and spoke honestly, but I did not reciprocate.

I just stood in silence ruminating, while she quietly continued to look away and mumble, "I'm sorry."

The bed I got for her was far from Civic Center where she was waiting for someone who was going to bring her, her nightly fix of heroin. If she did not get her fix she would get violently ill out in the night and suffer misery and pain beyond what the elements could ever do to her. She would be up all night suffering, feeling like she was dying, and possibly literally dying, in the elements going through physical and mind wracking withdrawals followed by a morning so dope sick she would be incapable of functioning well enough to accomplish her survival routines. On the pyramid of needs, heroin was at the base, a bed and shelter above that.

I allowed my feelings to get in the way of being sensitive to her feelings and needs. I realized as much as I thought I knew about living with addiction and homelessness, I still had more to learn. My reaction was selfish. She took away my elation, my feel good high. I placed my emotions above hers, not meeting her where she truly was.

ERIC HOFSTEIN

SOPHIA

On a mid-December Sunday my beat partner and I were working as lunch relief for the other team who were taking advantage of a quiet moment to warm up their food. Finding an opportunity to get a full meal instead of ping-ponging between oversized gulps of cold food and 911 calls was not something experienced patrol officers squandered. Twas the season of snatch and runs, and hot chocolate, when patrol officers get quickly buried in 911 calls for stolen gift bags left unobserved on platform benches, drunken patrons stumbling onto tracks, or fighting from platform to train, to platform again adding their seasonal donation of blood, vomit, and alcohol-fueled cheer to the BART holiday atmosphere.

Once I logged into the Automated Dispatch (CAD) computer system, I scanned the 911 calls among the half dozen districts and their fifty stations that speckled the BART tracks winding across the Bay Area. As I watched the call taker in dispatch type in new calls for service, I noticed a non-priority call placed into pending status for the other team to take after their meal break. The reporting party said her sister got a BART fare evasion citation, then lied during the detention using the reporting party's information. Now she was on the hook for her sister's crime. This was causing financial hardships, and she wanted a police report to press charges and clear her name.

I was curious about the suspect's backstory. Perhaps Sophia used her sister Johanna's name in vengeance for some previous slight or sibling rivalry. Maybe she was just another one of the thousands of homeless routinely committing low-level crimes throughout the city, using her sister's information because that is easier than trying to memorize a fabricated name. It could also be that there was something deeper and more significant than simple fare evasion and an angry sister in this scenario.

My curiosity was piqued. I read the details and saw Sophia and Johana were from an upper middle-class town in the East Bay Valley Station district. There was a dark side to the affluence in those communities that infested the youth and was spreading in my last days at the Sheriff's Office. I wondered if Sophia was one of those infected.

I called Johanna while the other officers were eating, something they would appreciate since they had other reports to catch up on. She answered the phone and I introduced myself as a BART officer working in the San Francisco stations. She thanked me for calling her back and said she wanted a police report and to press charges because of the devastating repercussions to her financial situation. She was anxious and desperate to get it resolved as quickly as possible since she was trying to buy a house for her family.

I told her I would write a police report, but it could take a few days for it to get to Investigations then assigned by the supervisor to a detective from there her case may sit in the detective's que for a long time before they would have time to address it as it was a low priority case. She sounded very upset, but I also heard the pain of love and loss in her voice when she invoked her sister's name. She said her sister was homeless in San Francisco and was using drugs.

With River still on my mind, I thought of a way to help Johanna speed up the process so I could alleviate her anxiety and pressure. It would be easier to get to her true feelings and thoughts about her sister's situation that way.

It was the weekend and none of the detectives were on duty, but I knew a one who wouldn't mind helping me out. We worked together as deputies in the jails and occasionally on patrol and had enough of a friendship for me to feel comfortable sending him a text about this situation on his day off. He was very dedicated to his work and had done some outreach work with me. He had personal experiences with a sibling who was a recovering addict. If drugs were a factor with Sophia, I knew he would do everything he could to help me help Johanna and her family. I sent him a text with the basic info and asked if he could help in any way.

A short time later he called me and we talked about the situation. I told him about the case and my feelings about the outreach aspect of it. I asked him if he could take a look at the video when he got to work the next day to expedite the criminal case, clear it or close it, so I could focus on any outreach work with the family. I'd complete the report right away and send it to him before the end of my shift so there would not be any delay.

I called Johanna back and gave her my usual set of informational instructions for fraud victims and included the report case number, my contact information for any questions, and explained the basics of how the police reporting process works. The detective would contact her when he got back to work the next day and at the end of the phone call, instead of an overly formal goodbye, I asked her about her sister more as a person than a suspect. Her tone changed as we spoke less about her sister's criminality and more about her family. Johanna opened up and vented her feelings like they had been building up to a critical point as she took me on a brief tour of their past. They were once very close, both victims of extreme abuse at the hands of their addict father who had severe mental health disorders. Johanna said Sophia took the role of a substitute parent and in her mind, had raised her like a father.

Suddenly she uttered a hitched, "I miss my Sophie." I could hear the emotional plea for her sister in her voice as strongly as in the words she used.

She explained how the trauma of their childhood caught up to them as young adults, and Sophia became a cliché as she fell into an abusive and dangerous relationship with a troubled boyfriend. She had a child with him and fell deeper into a self-destructive life of drugs and petty crime, peaking when they burglarized the family home. This was a breaking point for their mother and was the final nail in the coffin for family cohesion. Sophia was essentially kicked out of the home and could not take her young son with her. She spiraled into a life of homelessness and addiction, her son now being raised by her mother.

Johanna still felt hurt and completely alienated from her sister while their young sons grew up together like brothers, a constant reminder of their family destruction and a sister, a daughter, a mother lost. No one in the family, including Sophia's little boy, had heard from her for about six months now. The fraud case was the only sign of life they received in that time, and now they were all frightened for her as the anger from past had time to dissipate.

I listened to Johanna's story and an old familiar tone I've heard many times over the years responding to calls for family disputes, domestic violence, and child abuse bubbled to the surface. It is a tone tinged with a pleading to stop the pain, return their love to one that was normal and healthy. In family abuse, love and pain become intertwined and indistinguishable, building years' worth of psychic injury that bleeds over into every relationship and social connection to others tainting their how family members love others and themselves. From someone who hurts us, what we recognize as love causes emotional turmoil, a cycle between anger and love back to anger. In this state of mind, I heard her defending her own emotions to herself as much as she tried to justify them to me.

Johanna sounded tired and strained and was crying more *for* her sister than *about her* sister. I knew I was not going to learn anything more that would help me find Sophia and try to get her connected to services, so I steered the conversation to a conclusion. Johanna said she really didn't want to press charges and only wanted to fix the financial issues and for her sister to get help. I wanted to end the call hanging on hope and not the raw emotions that were clearly hard for her to express, so I told her I would look for her sister and if I found her, I would offer her any help she wanted. I asked if she wanted to stay in the loop and reconnect and she said she and their mother both wanted that. She said her dream was to one day see Sophia reunited with her little boy.

Sophia was on the same path as River, having walked away from family living a life that mirrored River's, full of shame and guilt compounded from the traumatic experiences women suffer when homeless and addicted, and the behaviors they adopt for the sake of physical and emotional survival. No one wants to be the most damaged person in the room, and if there is no hope for a "normal" life ever again, it's easy to give up and give in.

I did not know if Sophia was a victim of sexual assault before she fell into her addiction, but I know River was. She told me how she was a student at a state college when she was raped at a party. Her life spiraled as she started to medicate the trauma from that assault, eventually getting addicted to opiates and heroin. Once on the streets she was raped again more than once falling into a common cycle for homeless addicted women. They are trapped in a Catch-22 cycle of trauma and self-medicating that spirals until it feels impossible to pull out. I quickly learned that on the street, 100% of women are raped. One young lady who was like a daughter to me shared that easily 90% of women are pimped, and many of those are *guerilla pimped.* Sexual trauma is medicated with street drugs that lead to more sexual trauma.

This compounds shame, and guilt, dwindles self-worth, balloons self-loathing, and reaches a point where hope or will for a normal life is dashed.

As a deputy, I took missing person's reports for young girls in Contra Costa County who ended up being trafficked into prostitution in Oakland, one county over. I saw a trend with the young girls who were targeted for having a certain type of personality and family background. The traffickers, the pimps, knew how to find them on social media, identify them at parties, hunt them at group events. The girls would be brutally raped and dehumanized, usually pumped full of drugs for days and even weeks until their spirit was broken beyond repair. Their Jekyll destroyed and the only hope they saw for a life full of shame, guilt, and pain was to sell themselves believing that their families would shun them or look at them in a way they could not tolerate. Any life they'd dreamt of having was no longer an option for them. They saw themselves as tainted so that no one other than their pimp would want them.

The longer Sophia was on the streets, the more likely she was to be assaulted and pushed deeper into the abyss. River pulled herself out despite the shame and guilt of facing her parents after her downfall. Unlike River, Sophia had also left behind her little boy. The additional trauma of facing abandonment of a child for homelessness and drugs. Many of the homeless women faced this situation alone, giving up on the hope of being a mother again and leaving family to raise their children. It sounds cruel, but the pain of cutting off a limb is more tolerable than allowing a gaping wound to fester. Women who are relegated to the streets know this trade off too well.

As I read through the emails that followed from Johanna and her mother over the next week, I learned Sophia's son missed his mother, but was doing his best to be a happy normal child. I knew her journey would affect him as much as her. It was a two-fer, save both or lose both. Many times as a deputy I had seen young children who lost a parent to drugs follow the same pathway as their dysfunctional parents. Sometimes there's sexual trauma, sometimes domestic violence, or drugs. Whatever the dysfunction there is always a price for that child to pay.

JIMMIE

One of the hardest aspects of patrol work in a city or town is feeling like a law enforcement version of a M.A.S.H. unit responding to emergencies that were often a result of years of family drama, perpetrated by adults who walked the Earth wrapped in cloaks of criminal behavior hewn out of their early trauma. Many times, calling 911 is a last-ditch act of pure desperation after all else has failed and there is an expectation that police officers are public servants to be used as a tool to resolve complex issues going back years, decades, or generations.

Earlier in my career, I worked inner-city gang-controlled neighborhoods where I watched generations of gang members fall from the innocence of childhood into that world. I saw them emerge street-hardened, cold, and apathetic to the things they once enjoyed and people they once loved.

Jimmie was a kid I met when he came riding his toy car down the street. His mom appeared, breathless from chasing him, lecturing him about being careful, like many rambunctious children too young to understand danger. The next summer I saw Jimmie sneaking around some trees as a homeless man popped out breathing heavily, upset, scanning left and right as he took off running. A split-second later Jimmie appeared from the same trees hot on the man's heels shooting at him with a pellet gun, laughing like a child playing a game of hide and seek. By the time Jimmie was ten years old he was committing armed robberies, targeting his neighbors in their driveways for their groceries and cash. By thirteen he formed a gang with his close friends to replace that of his father's generation, which had gone because they were all in prison or dead. By twenty Jimmie and his gang were swept up by the sheriff's office and FBI for over 30 charges across 12 cities including a home invasion, multiple freeway shootings, murders, car jackings, armed robberies, and drug dealing.

I watched many lives walk this 'birth-to-jail' pathway. I watched lives lost, lives wasted, lives that could have been different. We go into law enforcement to make a difference, but I couldn't change these lives. For some of these young people, I investigated parents who committed horrible sexual acts on their children; children they held at birth who at some point morphed into a deviant sexual fetish. I saw some of these kids grow up entering the cycle themselves as sexual deviants, most if not all using hard narcotics at an early age to numb the pain. I'd respond to calls for service involving them, hearing their names spoken by other officers and their peers over the years. I'd house childhood traumatized children when they became legal adults sometimes on my jail module, having to place them on the protective custody module where sex offenders and *snitches* were hidden from general population. Cousins who were close enough for frequent sleepovers and both grew to be murderers were finally pit against one another by their environment and tossed aside by society, one landing on my jail module, the other in the grave. A dark and sick cycle of life as inescapable for police officers as the victims and perpetrators by whom we were surrounded. We knew their stories, we knew their names, we saw their pain and always took at least a little piece of it home with us.

After the incident with Juana and my transfer to Valley Station I didn't know what to expect among the local youth. I had seen some of them on the jail modules for drugs and burglaries, but I did not know the circumstances and dynamics of their lives in the more affluent communities, unlike Jimmie's. It wasn't until Valley Station that I was really exposed to the pill use that became pervasive among the "rich kids."

In the beginning Xanax pills, a Benzodiazepine class of antianxiety drug sometimes called 'footballs' due to their elongated football-like shape, were most common. By the time I left the sheriff's office for BART, pill addiction had taken a sudden and more sinister turn as the powerful opioid Oxycontin made its rise to the top. When I met Jason, he was a baby-faced adolescent. Dirty and covered in scabs, he confided in me that when he was ten years old, he took his grandmother's Xanax pills for pain, his self-prescribed medication. When her

Xanax was no longer sufficient, he began swapping pills out for stronger results, until eventually the street dealers became his pharmacy.

As addiction to Oxycontin spread throughout the communities in the Valley Station area, residential burglaries increased proportionally. I recognized patterns to the burglaries, which also coincided with an uptick in burglaries and thefts at pharmacies, pointing to a clear motive of pill seeking. I was getting dispatched to burglaries in wealthy communities where the same patterns emerged: expensive and easily concealable items like jewelry were untouched, only the bedrooms and bathrooms were ransacked, and the occupants were elderly or infirmed with chronic and debilitating conditions like cancer that ensured a lot of pain medications would be found in the home.

Soon another pattern emerged: the more they stole the more they decompensated. We'd contact them on a traffic stop or see them walking down a street, and the rapid decline of their physical appearance and mental acumen was startling. The fall from sharp witted high school kids to burned out addict young adult was hard and fast. It was at that point their groups fell apart and turned on each other, getting into conflicts, and even targeting each other as and their own families for burglaries. With their growing addiction came a desperation and sloppiness to their thievery resulting in more arrests, probation, parole, and expulsion from their families. As cases made their way onto court calendar, they'd turn on each other for leniency in sentencing.

Some, finally sick of where they had fallen to in life, got cleaned up and sober. Many didn't and ended up alone, bitter, addicted, and homeless.

We got to know them fairly well, their families, social groups, habits, and quirks. The primary leader and the most prolific narcotic addicted burglar of them, and one of the longest lasting ones who seemed to enjoy the lifestyle, was a well-known charismatic high school athlete who graduated and according to him, moved on to do some work as a model.

He was elusive after graduating high school and the daytime burglaries took a sudden significant uptick. I tracked him down and confronted him, letting him know I knew what he was up to. The burglaries stopped.

Confident of my theories, I went to his home in the heart of an exclusive neighborhood known for its millionaire residents. His mother shared that she had spent hundreds of thousands of dollars on expensive substance abuse rehabilitation facilities in southern California and other states only to have him quickly relapse. Her home was worth a million or more, yet she was running out of money. She leveraged her mortgage to pay for private rehabs that didn't work. She was cash poor and going totally broke. She eventually had a violent falling out with her son filing for a combination eviction and restraining order. She could not and would not help him anymore, she was done with him and said jail was what he needed.

There was an underlying trend with some of the affluent families; some sacrificed family for lifestyle, some lost their children to the influences of their wealthy friends who lived for the excesses that money and drugs provided. Others saw problems like mental health disorders at a young age and chose to ignore them, choosing instead to bet on the ability to spend their way out of mental illness, addiction, and dysfunction. I met families who lived in complete denial of major dysfunctions and criminal behaviors to devastating conclusions. One addicted and now in his twenties child from this same community would get arrested regularly and at every jail release his parents would be waiting for him in the jail parking lot with a new expensive car hoping they could essentially bribe him into stopping his drug use and criminal behavior. Addiction and criminality, and homelessness impartially equal opportunity.

ERIC HOFSTEIN

SOPHIA AND
THE KINGPIN

There was no boiler plate precedent to follow for this. No standards of care had been established, no peer recognized processes and procedures, no mentors from whom to seek advice. I would be on my own creating something new, not knowing what I did not know, venturing out into a new professional mission surrounded by an array of legalities and protocols I now had to navigate.

It was time to do the work, which I could not do if I could not find her. She likely had warrants like many homeless addicts committing crimes, so just walking up to her as a uniformed police officer in public might make her run or at least frighten her out of engaging with me for help. This was especially true if she had an addiction to feed that could be choked out in a dingy jail cell if I was there to arrest her. Cops often use subterfuge to accomplish their tasks and the homeless community often runs afoul of the police, making that community especially paranoid of officers.

Simply talking to a cop in public could cause irreparable harm. In the jails when inmates would approach me to ask questions, they always had what they called a *post*: someone with them at any police contacts to verify they weren't snitching. I had seen inmates lumped up for violating this street code and I knew in the drug fueled paranoia of the homeless community talking to Sophia in public could get her labeled a snitch. Beside potential for violence, she could be spurned by the drug dealers and peers which would be incentive enough to not talk to me.

None of this mattered if I could not find her. I searched for BART contacts with Sophia to see if she was "known to the BART system"; if she had regular contacts beyond that one of which I knew. Once I learned she was not a regular commonly in the BART system and known to officers from consistent contacts, my goal was to figure out her behaviors and haunts to predict where I was most likely to find her.

I knew I needed to learn about and dial in to the homeless communities the way I had done before in the jails and high crime neighborhoods. I used my seniority to get assigned to the Civic Center beat, the heart and soul of the San Francisco homeless community. I walked *top side* among the groups as much as inside the station itself. I watched the black market from a distance and how the groups interacted.

I learned how they grouped up and associated with each other. I paid attention to the nuances and quirks of individuals within the cliques in and around the BART stations. When I encountered them as a call for service, or proactively, I took a less officious approach than I otherwise would have. I learned where they were from, I listened to their stories, and I asked them to help me learn about their world. As much as I thought I knew, I learned more than I ever expected about their lives and the world they survived in. I was woefully unprepared for the level of trauma they suffered through; particularly those of the women.

I thought about the connections I had made within the community and how word of my work looking for River and others was starting to spread. I took what information I had on Sophia from her family into the tenderloin to seek help and information. Soon a respected person in the community approached me. He had cautiously watched me working with people, connecting them to family and services, and made a point of letting me know he was watching me and respected my work.

After I helped a couple with a child in his group of friends, he offered to help me. He had a lot of connections on the streets. I had seen him at night dealing fentanyl and heroin to the heavy users in front of the library across from city hall and the Graham theatre, but I had also seen him helping others. The steps and walled wheelchair ramps where he slung dope made him look like a drug kingpin from street level. He would lean on the low wall at the top, surrounded on both sides by gorked out users. His more alert spotters could easily examine from that high, unobstructed vantage point. Any raid by law enforcement would be thwarted by dumped baggies, fleeing suspects holding the main batch of dope, and mass chaos of those users who remained upright thinking they were the cop's target. None of this was my concern, or something to judge by my bias. I was not wearing my cop hat for this mission, and I needed his knowledge and assistance to find a missing needle in a haystack of 8,000 needles.

Without his help, she would still be in that haystack, languishing on the streets, her son never knowing what happened to his mother. I took off my cop hat, and it paid off. As I worked at finding a way to elicit his help, he approached me. He asked if I was still looking for Sophia. He pointed across the street towards the A.C.T. theatre and told me she would be walking down that street in about ten minutes. He had spoken with her. He had explained who I was. He had told her I was 'alright'. He had vetted me. She showed up, mired deep in a self-loathing only a mother who had left her child could know. She had no reason to believe there was a way back to her family, to her boy, when I found her.

Johanna drove the hour commute into the city to meet with Sophia, to bury hatchets and repair bridges. The family was healing. By now I knew that it was imperative to have anything she needed ready to match Sophia's timing and motivation. I needed a plan to reintroduce her to her child, and to build her confidence for that first contact. After Sophia's mother consulted with her son's therapist to ensure that my approach was appropriate, I was able to facilitate that first phone call and help her explain her absence, so he did not self-blame like children do. *Mommy was sick and had to live in San Francisco where her medicine was, she was too sick to call and did not want to get him sick. But she was getting better.*

Our conversations about her son served two purposes: they not only reminded her of their bond and of her place in his life, but that there was still a place for her. She shared with me his love for sharks. I reminded her the significance that his mommy loved him well enough to hold in her heart the things about which he cared. Meanwhile, I had my wife purchase a small stuffed shark, and I had Sophia write a little note on it for him. I brought it back home to the East Bay and we mailed it off to him.

Her sister sent me photos of his reaction and I shared them with her. Sophia's eyes widened, tears welled, her hand reflexively clasped over her mouth as she looked at the picture her sister sent to my phone. Her son was embracing the shark like a life preserver, her handwritten note on the packaging. His face alight with happiness, the smile betraying the joy of a child who never once blamed his mother for having to leave. That was the smile of a boy who was ready for mommy to come back into his life.

Mommy was getting better. She called me for a

phone cord, which enabled her to be in nightly contact with her son, almost as if it had been routine all along. City endorsed tent camp. Services. The next time I saw her she had taken all the resources I gave her and took initiative that shocked me. She had gotten on Suboxone to aid in her recovery and had secured a job interview. Housed. The last time I saw her she was well dressed, happy, healthy, and on the BART platform with a new bike, on her way to an appointment.

BEAT CHECK

alk the beat with me. I want to introduce you to a few more.

Tim Blevins, the quintessential sad tale of genius and talent destroyed by addiction and the subsequent fall from grace into homelessness. Despite the documentaries and occasional public attention, when I saw Tim performing in the BART station halls he was always alone. No fans, no adoring crowds, no agents waited for him to finish to move on to the next gig.

Tim was gifted with a powerful baritone voice that made its way through the halls from Juilliard to off Broadway classics like Porgy and Bess. His agent once told my partner Dave Touye that he was an amazing talent, but his demons were more powerful than his voice and he grew addicted to women and alcohol. Tim fit that old cliché; always happy, engaging with everyone who spoke to him. Perched on the tiny seat of his walker clutching his microphone, his huge, disarming smile was always there to greet us. "How are you today,

Tim?" We always knew the answer. He was always in pain from a damaged hip, but the money raised by a sympathetic public to get him surgery never panned out, so he continued to perch here for years doing what he loved most for an audience of commuters and his fellow homeless. As Dave said, "I think he was comfortable where he was, even though he was in a lot of pain, it felt like something he was in control of. Even if it meant he wasn't getting better."

We once saw him sitting on his walker, sleeping by the ticket machines below Civic Center Plaza where the black market thrived and the addicted came and went to trade stolen goods for drug money or to find a spot to smoke and shoot up. He gripped his microphone close to his face with one hand and clutched a handful of dollar bills in the other, with more bills scattered on the floor in front of him. I saw his lips moving in silence, interrupted by the occasional grin. It looked like he was performing in his sleep. We woke him up and told him he was sleeping with his earnings exposed. He smiled and laughed.

Dave asked, "What were you dreaming of?"

Tim responded, "I was performing.

"Oh yeah? How'd you sound?"
Tim beamed back at Dave, "I sounded good."

Raff wandered the streets for five years, the city

bureaucracy refusing to give him the diagnosis he deserved. Once he was medicated for his schizophrenia, he was home with family, with a job, a bank account, ecstatic with the privilege of mundanity.

Sakura was usually naked and violent. For several years, she was unwilling, and unable to seek help, her Japanese parents at a loss for how to navigate the system. Dave and I had to fight on her behalf. She is back home, even if she is with her adoptive human parents from Saturn. She likes them now. Even so, the Japanese consulate sent Dave cookies and a thank-you.

Aaria is the eighty-eight-year-old ballet dancer, daughter of a famous painter cut off by family. An Australian national discarded by her American husband unknown years ago, languishing on BART trains in her own waste. "The system" insisted she was fine, argued her agency, ignoring her advancing dementia. Dave fought on her behalf to convince her social worker of her dire need, and she is flourishing in a respite home.

Nina, with autism and a history of sexual trauma, was written off as "a drug user." She was discharged after brain surgery, not yet healed and unable to care for herself. Social Services argued that she was fine and wrote her off. I fought for her and helped her mother to advocate for her. Together we bucked the system who would abuse the concept of a person's agency to their detriment. She is finally safe and well.

Tree Top simply needed someone to see him. He needed to be seen as anyone other than another black crackhead. Then, he helped himself.

Daniel never made it off the street. But he wasn't assaulting people every day. He wasn't throwing his colostomy bag regularly. He even thanked me. Out of respect for me and the relationship we forged, he made a conscious effort not to cause issues in the BART system. More importantly he taught me to manage my expectations, and that success is relative. That is the meaning of harm reduction.

Many have shared with me in honoring the young CHP officer Kenyon Youngstrom who gave his life on a dirty freeway protecting the public. Many honored with me the opera singer Tim Blevins as he shared his talent with the commuters and fellow addicts on the dirty floors of a city train station. And every time I think of them a wave of guilt washes over me, as my thoughts are drawn to the other stories that will never be honored or mourned by a loving family or adoring fans. They will only be remembered by me and a few other first responders. We were their last connection to a humanity from which they lost membership. We were 911, emergency, the last bastion of civilization.

Their histories are only known by me. I think of the thousands more in that one American city whose stories will never be known to anyone. They will blink in and out of existence like shadows on society. Parents, children, siblings, impoverished, the formally affluent, the well-educated, professionals, teachers, and talented artists suffering a slow demise for no reason other than the biology they inherited or string of lived circumstances: their unfortunate roll of the dice.

No matter how much I try to move on, my thoughts drift back to a shared moment with each of them that will die with me. I see images of a city or train station on the news and suddenly find a chunk of my day was lost in memories and I will emerge from it feeling a loss I can't articulate.

All I can do now sitting here in the quiet of retirement is to share pieces of my thoughts and memories hoping others will feel enough to picture the loss of life on the streets right outside our front doors. These lives fade away unseen and ignored. This world few care to know about beyond skirting around the sleeping lump on a sidewalk or the alcoholic propped up outside a 7/11, a crumpled and dirty Big Gulp cup in hand hoping for eye contact with a plea for the change they need for their cheap alcohol. Knowing that the sad tale they spin for spare change will be a lie, so you avert your gaze pretending to not see them. Maybe you feel guilty thinking 'better that poor bastard than me' and drop the coins, but deep down you know that was more for you than for them.

After all my years of helping victims, investigating crimes, doing outreach and having some successes in bringing the down and out back into the world, I still wonder how they got there, and what could have changed their fate. Those thoughts don't go away, ever.

I hope others would afford me what I needed if I ended up watching the world from which I fell passing me by day after lost day, as I languish trapped in the bell jar. This is where my guilt lives. I am always painfully aware of how so many of us are just one check, one illness, one happenstance away from a dive into the abyss hoping someone will reach down and hold out a steady hand to help us pull ourselves back out to join the world once again.

ERIC HOFSTEIN

END OF WATCH 2021-03-17 1800

17:25:03: "Got a man down! Need some Narcan!"

17:25:45: My partner crouches by the victim, "One deployed."

"I got a second if you need it."

"Gimme that."

17:26:02: "I got a Code 33 on this channel," into my radio. "Is he taking any breaths at all?" To my beat partner. We discuss his breathing and pulse.

I ask, "Is he taking any breaths at all...No radial [pulse]."

Audible breath.

"There we go! We got liftoff!"

Agonal breath.

Agonal breath.

17:26:59 I revert to full EMT mode, instructing my

beat partner to rub the victim's back to stimulate him.

"C'mon man!" his peers try to cheer him on.

17:27:17 I scan the crowd as I explain the next steps to my partner. I see Friedrich. Strange name for a Black kid from Tennessee. Eight years in California and addicted to tar heroin. He was in the city funded tent camp. He was one of my helpers, assisting me when I was looking for other contacts. He was very friendly, engaging with me, apparently with no qualms talking to a uniformed cop in full view of his peers. He had asked me to help him find his mother. He had given me his family contact information. Now I saw him, knowing I had not been able to look for his mother. I had not been able to put in my usual exhaustive effort to look for his mother because I had been preparing to leave. I had not told him that I was leaving him and others seemingly suddenly, without warning, in the hands of a fledgling outreach unit with strangers who had neither the complicated relationships with stakeholders, nor personal emotional investment in their individual success.

Now Friedrich sees me. He leans on a metal barricade as he watched me work for this stranger's life. The guilt compounded as I strained to keep the victim's airway open.

We're losing him again.

Agonal breathing. We struggle to keep his airway open. The Narcan can't work if he doesn't move it through his bloodstream. He can't move it through his bloodstream adequately if he doesn't breathe.

"There we go! Alright. I can feel a pulse now. Yeah, he's got a pulse now." I don't realize it at the time, but my tone is almost celebratory.

"Second time!" I hear the shout from the small crowd of his friends.

The victim stirs.

I check his belly to see if he's breathing deeply enough for it to count. His belly is rigid. I only see shallow respirations. His pulse is weak and tachycardic. I'm still concerned about his airway.

17:31:44 I hear the first *whoop whoop* of EMS.

I give report not unlike an EMT. Four rounds of Narcan. Eight milligrams total. I watch as EMS rolls him away.

17:35:54 it's over.

Now Fentanyl-fueled, the opioid epidemic washing over the city spills another victim onto the shore at the feet of EMS.

Friedrich approaches me. Time to face the music.

Friedrich tells me that the victim had just had a bad encounter with family and hinted that this overdose was a suicide attempt. Friedrich anxiously clings to me as we walk and talk, and it weighs on me. It is all over, and I don't tell him I couldn't help him, and I feel like a coward who betrayed him.

I return to the station, clean out my locker. I stare at my aged nametag, slightly peeling from its place for a moment. It hits me. I remember looking at my locker for the first time when my name was *FNG, boot*. Now, twenty-seven years later, I make my final *10-7* broadcast. There is no goodbye, no party, there are no after-shift drinks. I close my locker for the last time, I go to the home I've been renting from Dave who walked me onto this path six years ago and beat me to retirement by a couple of years, pack my last belongings into my Camry and point it east to meet my wife and children who went ahead six months ago.

The trip takes a week, and I'm driving alone. There is a lot of time to think, to remember, to plan next steps.

ERIC HOFSTEIN

EPILOGUE

I was privileged to have had over 130 one on one personal interactions, connections, out of the hundreds I met but never got to know. Those out of the over 8,000 people in one tiny metropolis of one state in this one country. I was honored to share with these people their journeys, their pain, and their victories in a way I never have before professionally or personally. I am compelled to share their stories before they are lost with the forgetfulness of age or go with me to my grave. I feel obligated to be their voice, advocating for them one last time.

We are fixated on homelessness. It would be convenient if the homeless were simply people without a place to sleep. The time for the convenient escape of finger-pointing must end. Empathy is not restricted by profession or political ideology. There are at least as many conservative "pull-yourself-up-by-your-bootstrap" people who are willing to forgo what they consider luxuries if it means their neighbors will be afforded essentials as there are liberal "everyone-needs-a-chance" people who vow never to help another again (and often keep that vow!) after haphazardly and naively giving in to someone's Hyde and suffering the consequences. The raw truth is that each of us must have a part in dismantling the present paradigm.

It is imperative that we understand that the issue at hand is not finding an end to homelessness entirely. There are as many reasons to be homeless as there are people on the street. It is naive to believe that there could ever be one solution to everyone's problem, yet that is the current method used by bureaucracies to combat homelessness.

There is no amount of money that will end this scourge. These numbers win elections, they don't improve lives. Housing first wins the hearts and minds of voters, but it is shocking how much easier it is to adjust to life on the street than it is to readjust to life indoors. In San Francisco, the vast majority of people who are housed end up back out within 30 days.

It is a mistake to approach homelessness as one war to be won. That is a generations long fight. The very concepts of what causes homelessness predate the events that brought us to the crisis we see today. Add to that ideas about mental psychosis and Substance Use Disorder that are several decades behind the information neurological science has borne out again and again, and it's quickly apparent that we are not only groping in the dark, we are doing so willingly, our hand on the switch we are unwilling to flip.

There is a new approach to the current crisis. We

must concentrate on the individual, each battle must be fought with fervor and won independently. Homeless people are not a monolith.

It would be more palatable if we were simply speaking about people who were without housing. Life is not that simple. There are layers to the human condition. We must talk about these people, yes. We must also talk about those on the precipice, at risk of becoming homeless. We must include those who are presently housed but are at high risk of returning to homelessness. We must not forget those who did not come to the streets with psychosis or addiction, but who were escaping, trafficked, or discarded. We must confront the needs of those so accustomed to the life they have created that reintegration is too high a hurdle. All are intertwined and inseparable.

We must speak of those left behind. It is counterintuitive to think of families and support networks as abandoned. It is people on the streets who are left behind by society. However, the pain of losing someone to the streets is real and must be addressed. Families and support networks have been discarded by people who have taken a path impossible to follow. The homeless are lost, figuratively and often literally. They have eked out a life for themselves, however precarious, in a place we cannot know. The crucial connections of past and present must be recognized and mended wherever possible.

We must bring more stakeholders to the table. This

is everyone's responsibility. We put it at the feet of the politicians, who pass it around to the medical doctors, psychiatrists, and social workers. These participants all come with important caveats.

First, each of them requires a level of professional distance from the subjects they serve. This is why they employ street-level caseworkers like San Francisco's HOT (Homeless Outreach Team) and lean heavily on civilian nonprofits like Fulton House and Glide Memorial Church. As I learned very early on, this arms-length approach is untenable. There is a risk to the rescuer, but if we're not willing to take the risk to help others, then there is no point.

Second, they are financially driven. The system is driven by city and state budgets and grants that are success-driven. The definition of success, however, is in the eyes of the grantee. One can be successful with the same individual every day in a given week. Each success is a dollar sign for the grantee. There is no impetus to solve the problem, and every motivation to allow a revolving door to develop. Conversely, without these grants, the work cannot continue, and no one gets help. This must change.

Third, as is the way with bureaucracies, the structure is rife with gatekeepers, jealously protecting their reputation and status. City and state governments want bone fides. Common wisdom suggests this guarantees results. To this end they throw money and the keys at people who sit in ivory towers with several letters behind their names to make decisions about the lives of people who are eating literal trash. These highly educated stakeholders sit at the table using the latest in inclusive language. They make note of words and phrases that are offensive and buzz words that say nothing new but are somehow important to insert into conversation, and thirty minutes into a one-hour monthly meeting they go around the room to discuss the successes they've identified, pat themselves on the back, and solve absolutely nothing.

I sat at the edge of that table, distressed because a young lady I was working with had shared with me her sexual assault story and I wanted to warn others that there was a serial rapist among their clients. I was shut down. This young lady was younger than my youngest daughter. I used the word "girl" when referring to her. Then I used the word "rape" to describe the trauma she'd endured. I was admonished: she is a woman, not a girl. My language was demeaning. There may be sexual assault survivors in the room. I must be mindful of their triggers. I made the mistake of believing I was in a room full of professionals whose primary focus was the vulnerable young men and women we were meant to be discussing.

These gatekeepers didn't want me at that table. I was a cop. Cops are bad. Cops have no empathy. Cops just want to paint everyone with one brush and make arrests. A caseworker with the HOT team was seen in a photograph with me that accompanied an article about the work I was doing. Not only did he get reprimanded, but a mandate came down to the entire team that they were never to work with law enforcement, despite their involvement in the Law Enforcement Assisted Diversion Program, with whom I worked tirelessly.

This brings me to my final point. There are no stakeholders, no outreach efforts, no organizations professionally trained in urgent and emergent situations that are in the field when these people are in the most need. These people work nine to five, Monday through Friday with holidays off. First responders are not only available twenty-four hours daily, but the police are always there, on the beat, with the people on the street. They see these people. They know these people. They see them when they are hitting a dose, they see them when they are boosting to make money to score.

When mom from Ohio comes looking for Joe in the Tenderloin district of San Francisco, who might know Joe, have seen Joe, or know Joe's associates? We go into their homes when their parents call us desperate. We see the family photos, learn the family history. People call on us at their wit's end to bring their families together, yet somehow, we are denied the opportunity to help after things have gone awry. There is no one more suited to forge relationships and build bridges to services. Instead, it is civilians who paint law enforcement with a broad brush, assuming we don't have the capacity to do the work necessary. We're already in the muck with them. We certainly have the facility to bring one or two out with us. Dave and I did it. It's being tried in police departments around the country. If they had the right tools, buy-in from the community and partners, there's no reason they couldn't replicate my work. If there are police officers willing to attempt the work with no outside support, imagine what we can accomplish when you give us a seat at the table.

---

[i] Callanan VJ, and Davis MS. in their article <u>Gender differences in suicide methods</u> in *Soc Psychiatry Psychiatry Epidemiol.* 2012

ACKNOWLEDGEMENT

We would like to thank the team of allies who stayed in the fight with Eric without whom there would be no successes. Nicole Brooks, Jessie Jones, and Jason Norelli, for allowing me to act as a voice for the voiceless.

David Touye was Eric's beat partner. He introduced him to the people that pulled hm into this work and walked this path with him for as long as he could.

Angela Averiett, the supervisor supreme who supported Eric went to bat for him even when his work wasn't popular.

Melissa Jordan and Mallory Moench believed in Eric writing articles about his work before they even knew they would be published.

Finally, we offer our gratitude to the more than 130 people who honored Eric by giving him the opportunity to share in their journey.

ABOUT THE AUTHOR

Mary Beth Haile And Eric Hofstein

Mary Beth and Eric are paying forward the gifts afforded them by the people they met in San Fransicso to continue the work with a new non profit.